10,000 Miles to Go
An American Filmmaking Odyssey

A Conversation with Filmmaker

Jason Rosette

Edited by William J. Grabowski

Copyright © 2016, 2017, 2018 and beyond by Jason Rosette

All Rights Reserved. ISBN: 9781983068720

CONTENTS

	Introduction	2
1	Street Smart	Pg 8
2	Working in the Public Forum	Pg 32
3	Film School of Hard Knocks	Pg 36
4	Ferlinghetti's Anarchist	Pg 43
5	The Camera Eye	Pg 51
6	Super 8 Archaeology	Pg 58
7	The Art Buffet	Pg 65
8	Quest for Gear	Pg 73
9	Naked Lunch	Pg 85
10	Sociological Warfare	Pg 92
11	Off-Season	Pg 99
12	Truth Versus Fiction	Pg 115
13	Showdown!	Pg 124
14	Cafe of the Outside	Pg 148
	Appendix 1- Recommendations	Pg 169
	Appendix 2- Photos and Media	Pg 178
	Bio	Pg 204

"As you set out on your journey to Ithaca,

pray that your journey be a long one,

filled with adventure, filled with discovery.

Laestrygonians and Cyclopes,

the angry Poseidon--do not fear them:

you'll never find such things on your way

unless your sight is set high, unless a rare

excitement stirs your spirit and your body."

– Homer, The Odyssey

"...I have seen the Venus Aphrodite

armless in her drafty corridor.

I have heard a siren sing

at One Fifth Avenue."

– Lawrence Ferlinghetti, A Coney Island of the Mind

INTRODUCTION BY THE EDITOR

"This filmmaker has presence, a restless curiosity stamped indelibly into his movies, writing, music and artwork", I thought, when I first discovered an old VHS tape of his work in a box of used books. This presence is not, as I would learn, tainted by the bluster of many post-twentieth century directors whose grasp of technique, history, and self-control is as shaky as their use of "found footage," CGI, and frequent references to fellow 'auteurs'. In his first award winning feature, BookWars ('Terrific'-LA Times) , the tape of which I'd unearthed by chance on that rainy Pennsylvanian day, Rosette's narration evokes memories of Rod Serling's suave menace, and Jack Webb's 'just-the-facts' deadpan tone (remember Dragnet?)-his laughter, though, belies such facile comparisons.

10,000 Miles to Go: An American Filmmaking Odyssey covers one filmmaker's trials and triumphs while travelling around the USA, just at the millennium's cusp, in search of equipment during the making his first grossly underfunded first feature. It is also a chronicle and expression of what many of today's bootstrappers and entrepreneurial types–in all fields–could encounter, to some degree, as they pursue their own particular dreams, ambitions, and explorations without much in the way of financial backing, safety nets, or safe words for that matter.

Some of this book's transcriptions, provided as recorded responses to my interview questions, are elliptical, out of a desire to preserve nuance, and necessity (natural pauses in speech, corrections, retractions, etc.). That cadence and style, the ellipses, also reminds us of a mutual admiration for the style of novelist Ferdinand Céline's (Journey to the End of the Night) books. Like Céline's, Rosette's achievements are the result of acts of will. No one held his hand or stuffed his bank account with greenbacks. Unlike Céline, however, Rosette is not bitter or cynical about some less-than-optimal experiences that would break more tender souls, and talks about them like lessons from the School of Hard Knocks. And he moves on.

So: how did I come to know this filmmaker and to edit this book?

In early 2000 my mother died. Several weeks later my employer at the time, a giant bookstore chain where I was working, let me–and many others–go for the 'long walk' (the entire 1970s-style mall was demolished). Then came 9/11, and a televised apocalypse baptized America. A mere three weeks later my father died in Ohio, and I wasn't there for him. You could say I was starting to sag under the weight of that fateful triumvirate, yet I had to carry on, as we all must do. So I stuffed it all away, tried to pretend that life was normal–ah, lethe!–and to move on from the unwinding coil of my life.

However, though I could run, I could not hide. In 2002 I got divorced, and moved into a small bunker-like apartment in Irwin, Pennsylvania. Everything sat in boxes. There, for the first time in the course of two sledge-hammer years, I was forced to pause, to confront things. What I had not done was allow myself to grieve–for my parents, my broken marriage, and all the victims of September 11 across the globe. Let's say I was not in the best of moods. If not for the novel I was writing, or attempting to write at the time...well...I had no intention of ending it all and becoming a pathetic literary cliché.

I decided that some physical action would break the spell. Unpacking some forty boxes of books one day-boxes which had sat, sagging ruefully, in the corner since my arrival in the small flat-I stumbled upon an old VHS tape. I dimly recalled seeing it before-or had I? That was one of the few times in my life that actually recall having a strong deja-vu experience.

The tape had one word scrawled in black on the peeling label: BookWars.

Then I remembered, yes, it had actually happened, it was not just a deja-vu. One fine drunken night, some months before, a friend had told me about this movie. It was a real life story that followed the lives of guys selling used books on the streets of New York City. OK, that seemed pretty straightforward. But then my friend had said it was more than that; it was, according to him, a sort of streetside 'epic'. True, his enthusiasm may have been heightened by cheap sangria, but in any case I jammed-with permission!-the VHS tape into a coat pocket, and it ended up on one of my shelves . . . fairly forgotten until that fateful day. In desperate need of something to uplift me, I beheld this odd and magnetic movie. My friend said it was a charmed story-not 'charming' but 'charmed'. I think those were the words he used. Whatever. He'd led me to some great books, but his taste in movies was... uneven. Into my crappy TV/VCR combo went the tape.

Over the next two days, I think I watched BookWars three or four times. It was a simple enough premise at first, it seemed. These fellows were selling used books from tables set up on the sidewalks in New York City. It was low budget, definitely an indie film, not Hollywood fare. It was extremely likeable right off the bat. At first, I couldn't decide what I liked best: pointing out to myself how many of the books being flashed on screen I actually owned, or watching the demographic spectrum of passing New Yorkers engaging, enraging, and sometimes ignoring the rogue's gallery of vendors. But what really brought it all to a satori flash point for me were some "hidden" aspects–things the movie did not literally spell out. The booksellers and their tables on the street seemed like a metaphor for something. It was as if there was something else behind the movie, something that lay latent–as if the story were a coded invitation of some sort, and the booksellers on screen were from another era. BookWars was jazzy, strange, honest, and wry at the same time. Frankly, watching this show made me feel good again–at that time, no easy task. I felt restored, able to function on all cylinders.

And for that reason alone, I remember the movie well.

I watched the tape once more. As it was playing, just as I decided I had to somehow connect with this Jason Rosette fellow, my ancient combo VHS player died. I decided to leave the tape tangled and forever entombed, in situ, within. Nonetheless, I saw this as a sign. My gut told me there was something there behind the movie that needed to be examined right away.

I tracked down the film's website and sent an email. After a few weeks, I had heard nothing back. I sent another about a month later. Still nothing. Finally, I'd gotten sidetracked with a new writing project, and had momentarily forgotten about it all, as things happen when life takes over. And, as it also it just so happens, the moment something is forgotten is the precise moment it appears again. That's when I finally heard back. The filmmaker apologized–it was something mundane, his web host had changed and his emails were delayed; something like that. A lengthy back-and-forth soon ensued. I watched the filmmaker's other works–more movies, but also various writing, music, and photography–and found elements in them as noteworthy as those in BookWars.

I assembled a list of questions and emailed them intermittently, and he responded by recording his answers and sending them back to me as MP3s. I found this to be interestingly reminiscent of the narration as it can be heard in his movie.

With a bit of editing based on those raw audio responses, this book is the result.

To quote Céline: "Experience is a dim lamp, which only lights the one who bears it."

In Rosette's case we're fortunate that the lamp also illuminates for others a winding path...and in doing so manages to educate, warn, inspire and entertain anyone curious enough to listen.

–William Grabowski, Editor

1. STREET-SMART: DISCUSSION WITH THE BOOTSTRAPPING FILMMAKER

From most accounts, BookWars is a film that had a painful birth. Beyond that, filmmaker / producer Jason Rosette seems to be a natural adapter to tough conditions and circumstances–a valuable trait in any director. But BookWars is a unique and unusual movie shot mostly in New York City. Executing and delivering the project required from the young director not only physical and emotional fiber, but a mix of street-smarts and diplomacy in America's most diverse demographic.

No delicate auteur, Rosette was a sidewalk bookseller in New York for several years before he took up the camera to document the world of his fellow street booksellers. During shooting, he worked the streets selling books, and he used the funds from the sales of his books to initially fund the project.

Having viewed the film a number of times, I interviewed the filmmaker and asked if BookWars was as painful an undertaking as I perceived it to be.

What follows are adapted from Rosette's recorded responses to my questions, along with additional material, photos and insights.

* * *

"BookWars started very loosely as a sort of home movie that I was shooting at the bookstand for fun with a borrowed video camera", says filmmaker Jason Rosette.

"Shooting began just for fun initially, but also because I had some inkling that it might make for an interesting historical document in some form. I had been selling books on the streets of Manhattan in the mid 90's for a couple years, in between movie production gigs and various editing gigs, whatnot. It was a way to generate cash, but I also had a great affinity for books. And I had some idea that I would not be doing it forever and I thought, hey, it could be interesting to look at the videos one day. And maybe fascinating, because–you know how it is–sometimes you're immersed in an environment where you're working and it becomes second nature, so you don't really see it as being exotic or anything."

"This is where I was working, and so I thought, well, maybe one day it'll be fascinating or interesting. And, you know, once you're set up with the books you do have a lot of time to sort of hang out and talk and preen them. Certainly it was not difficult to shoot B-roll and footage of customers in the streets and other fellow booksellers after I had been set up. After you set up, there's time. The setting up and the breaking down is a more intense effort."

"The painful part of BookWars came near the end–the finishing, ironically. Actually, the painful part came in like, the final third, after I'd gone to San Francisco to work with the two co-producers there, the Montoya brothers [James and John], who really helped out a lot. They did a lot of the heavy lifting. By that I speak figuratively. It was their machine, their Media 100 machine, I primarily used."

"As mentioned, at the time, one reason it was so challenging to make BookWars was because it originated when the industry was going through a transition from linear editing to non-linear. It had transitioned, actually, to non-linear. Whereas now every computer, every laptop, comes with a movie editing program. Back then, desktop editing was confined to two systems, really: Avid and Media 100. Both were hardware-based. They had a dedicated graphics card which supported the video editing. You know, processors were not fast enough, not as fast as they are now, and there was not enough memory. The architecture of the machines could not support what we can do now. So, because of that, those machines were rather expensive to rent. An Avid, or a Media 100–to get time on those systems, you had to go in at night at a friend's machine, or some studio that you knew."

"It so happened that, well, the next step was I knew that I needed a Media 100 system. Or an Avid, to make BookWars. While I was fooling around making these home videos out at the bookstand, a documentary filmmaker I had known a bit from an internship I had worked on–I worked as an editing intern just for a day, actually, on this movie. I only worked for a day, because they wanted someone–this is New York City for you!–they wanted someone to work five days a week, for free. How can you sustain that? And separately, that ties into why I think a lot of artists left New York. Which is...you know, do a Google search, you'll find many articles about that."

The trend of the unpaid internship has become even more acute at the time of this writing in early December of 2015. Even so, the then-emerging filmmaker managed to make a crucial connection during his spectacularly brief internship.

"Anyway, I couldn't sustain the internship. I went to work for the first day, things worked out fine; they liked me, it's just that I couldn't afford to stay. But that's where I met Michel Negroponte, who's a documentary filmmaker in New York, and who would later happen upon me at the bookstand after I'd started to shoot some video there as a sort of proto-version of what the movie would eventually become.

Luckily that one day of contact, that one day of internship, came to something. I didn't leave the internship because I was flaky. It was just because...well, they said, 'We need someone for four days a week.' Was it four or five? Even so, in Manhattan? Working for free? I don't know–I couldn't do it. I'm not from a wealthy background. I come from the Midwest, sort of working-class background, etc. I had a scholarship to go to NYU Film School–partial scholarship."

Did working on the streets require a certain mix of

literary "smarts," salesmanship, and diplomacy?

"Yes, it required literary smarts, which I gained after selling books for a while. They obviously improved my literary smarts; that faculty improved. So, I was out shooting sort of home movie style at the bookstand. Michel Negroponte happens to stop by the bookstand-you know, 'Hey, how you doing?' We were talking for a while, and he didn't know I was selling books. I wasn't doing it as a lark, or some kind of, you know, thesis study. I did it because I was pretty broke and needed a way to generate cash in between gigs. As you can see in the movie it was suitable for that purpose, and I liked books, and I liked being out in the public forum, you know, and doing that kind of work."

"So, he mentioned, hey, why don't you develop it into more of a formalized documentary. And I thought about it, because at the time the movie could have gone in just about any direction-it could have become a sort of wacky, Clerks-like project, or as Michel mentioned, it could have become a nonfiction or documentary project. And I said, well, let me put something together that can stand on its own."

"By this time, I had started to grow a bit weary of

selling books for the season...well, every winter, of course, people would sort of stop selling books, or reduced the time they spent because it was just too cold. If there was a warm day, we'd come out. Generally speaking, people would pack up for that season. I think at that point I had decided, okay, winter's coming. Let me take the tapes I have shot already, and I'm going to go back down to New Mexico where I had spent some time before. That's where I edited my first drama, my first movie, Charlie's Box, which you can see on Amazon and some other platforms. And which I finished, basically, and funded with bookselling money, by the way."

"I had edited Charlie's Box down there on a flatbed, 16 millimeter, so I knew people down there. I worked on the Western [The Desperate Trail] in 1995, so I went down to New Mexico and I knew a guy named Alan Fulford who had a video studio. He was pretty laid-back, and he said, yeah, sure. I said, can I use your tape-to-tape editing system, to put together the first cut of BookWars?"

"Back then, it was tape-to-tape. Alan didn't have a non-linear system, and I didn't know anyone with one–but that was the best I could do. So I put those variables together, and said, okay, well since I'm packing up for the winter anyway, I'm going down to New Mexico and I'm going to put together an assembly edit at Alan Fulford's place, called Field and Frame. He's an associate producer on the movie. He helped; he contributed, you know, his tape-to-tape system.

So I went down there and put together the assembly edit of BookWars, the very first assembly edit. And we showed it at his studio workspace, on Super Bowl Sunday. I can't remember which year it was...1996? But there was a good crowd; it was pretty interesting to see it taking shape embryonically."

What was the next step? Did the filmmaker have an itinerary?

"From there, I didn't know what to do, because I was–I figured, I have to go to L.A, where there's a lot more equipment. And I was closer to L.A. at this point than New York...and let me see if I can find some gear to continue fleshing out this movie. I knew a guy from film school, who said come on out, there's some music videos and things I'm working on. I went out there. There was some work; there wasn't a lot. It seems like, in the business, there's often somebody who may be high on the totem pole who wants to build up a posse of friends to display to others. So, they might invite you to come out and work with them, but part of the reason–I think–is that they want a posse around for show. Sort of a hierarchical posse."

"And so I realized that later, oh yeah–there is some work here in L.A., but it's not mind-blowing. And I was still scraping to get by. I was living in this strange house in Venice with a gang of bongo players living in the cellar. I had a jalopy kind of beat-up car. I had to, you know, repair it myself and all that, and I'm amazed my repairs actually all worked out. I used a coat hanger once to jerry-rig a clip on a brake caliper because I had to get to Hollywood to pick up a check and my brakes were shot. I was able to get the new brake pads but didn't have the exact clips required for that car, I think it was an old Toyota or Datsun. Anyway, I did some work on commercials and music videos while looking for an Avid or Media 100 system.

There was some work, so I was working there–but not a lot."

The constant search for equipment was–as Rosette attests–a much bigger challenge during the late 1990s, even with fewer aspiring filmmakers than today clamoring for it. Regardless, he couldn't get the results he desired without finding the proper editing system.

"At that point, a friend of mine from high school days, she had gone on to do some acting and some B-movies and things. She knew these guys with a production studio in San Francisco, a little indie production studio, and they had a Media 100 system. She said, why don't you get in touch with these guys? So I got in touch with them; I sent them an audio cassette, actually, of me reading a narration. It's not from the movie that you see."

"The narration in the movie is derived from that original, longer writing and longer take. And they liked it. They liked the feeling of it, that sort of Beat spirit of it. I wasn't trying to be a gypsy or a bohemian or anything. The fact is, I was moving around because at the time I had to go where the editing system was. And so I'm trying to think back...if they had laptops back then, where you could edit on your own, and trying to imagine if I had Final Cut Pro back then I almost certainly would not have traveled to such far-flung places to make the movie."

Rosette found he must travel even more than anticipated, simply because he had to work wherever the equipment could be found. While this apparent restlessness might appear attractively free-spirited, it was simply a practicality. "It wasn't just on a lark," he flatly states. "It was also a necessity-I had to go where the equipment was. And so, these two brothers-the Montoya brothers, James and John-had a place called S.A.I.D. Communication. They said yeah, come on up, we'll work on it, we'll make a deal. We'll be the co-producers. And it became...that was the first real concrete pivotal step in getting the move into its final condition. Which meant that I had to go to San Francisco. I had to move there; I couldn't commute."

"So I went up there, with my beat-up Toyota-whatever it was-Corolla, at the time. A different Japanese car than appears in BookWars. Went up to San Francisco with a suitcase full of the original tapes, and loaded them onto the machine and started editing as much as I could. You know, 'Make hay while the sun shines' as, uh-who said that? It wasn't William Blake. Anyway, that old proverb."

How did he perceive San Francisco-considered, along with Silicon Valley, to be a 'bootstrapping' center of the United States?

"It was great. I mean, I was still not funded. I was still working out-of-pocket. So I was living in a pretty small, residential hotel. It was small but clean, in North Beach. Back then it was eighty five dollars a week. I went there recently, actually, and it was two thirty a week. Still not bad, but that was fifteen years ago. So, I moved into a residential hotel, not far from the editing studio, which was on the edge of Chinatown and Nob Hill, and spent as much time as I could hauling ass to edit and shape this movie. Really, with the Montoya brothers doing...they and Dennis Muldrow, who was one of the partners, he was a guy who worked at carpentry and construction by day. He would come back covered in sawdust, tired, and sit down and watch the cut. I mean, it was real heavy lifting. These guys, I have to hand it to them, they really...without them it would not have been made–let me put it that way. BookWars could not have been made. It would not be...it would not resemble what it is."

I ask how he managed to support himself while working with the Montoyas.

"Eventually, after a lot of editing, I got it to a pretty sharp point, the movie. And I was working then doing temp jobs, and I was working as a bicycle cab guy for cash, in Chinatown, on Fisherman's Wharf, sometimes on the weekends. I was doing editing jobs when I could find them, made some connections at BAVC (Bay Area Video Coalition) and got a few editing gigs that way. I did temp gigs...office work, whatever I could find. By this point it's 1999, and the cut is 90% there...but it still needs to be polished. I'd been in touch with Michel, the co-producer in New York, throughout this time. He would occasionally, you know, he would give some input."

Was Negroponte augmenting the budget?

"Not financially. He wasn't fundraising. He was basically providing some input on the cut and process. He was more like a coach, or casual advisor than a traditional producer. At some point later we formalized that he would be a co-producer also, so then we had four co-producers. Myself, the Montoya brothers, Michel Negroponte...and I expressed to him that it's pretty much done. You can see the cut. It was about 90% done. And at that point Michel found a contact, referred me to a contact. A couple of folks–documentary filmmakers in New York, who had a Media 100 editing system. I could come and use their machine–not for free, I had to pay...and I did, actually. But I could stay at the little studio as well. This was in the upper West Side of Manhattan."

Did Rosette really want to move–across the country–yet again?

"Would I want to come back to New York and push the movie to the next 'final' level? Some discussion ensued, and that was the decision I made. To go back and formally finish it, in New York. Do a few pick-up shots, move it from the current state it was in...the movie was about 90% complete in San Francisco, so the goal was to move it up to about the 100% mark. And the presumption was–the assumption was, on my part at least–that by collaborating with a somewhat well-connected documentary filmmaker, Michel, the opportunities to get the movie distributed and get it more widely seen, and so forth, would be enhanced. He was fairly well-connected in the documentary world, and so it followed that that was a reasonable assumption. He had been providing input throughout the process. Not doing heavy, producerly lifting like the Montoya brothers; as I said, Michel tended to offer positive 'coaching' and advice here and there. It was sometimes really, really tough...the 'down' periods that you ask about really occurred when I was in San Francisco struggling to push through the final edit to completion. Even so, looking back, some additional fundraising besides my own efforts would have reasonably been very welcome, since I was red-lining it already, doing all I could to survive and claw forward with the movie."

"Imagine...I'm working as a part-time bicycle cab driver at the Wharf, doing temp jobs, odd editing jobs, scraping money together to keep going. And, at one point, the Montoya brothers, they said they had to free up the machine for another project which was coming in. It was a project about strippers who form a union in San Francisco. One of the production team for that movie was a lady named 'Bill,' who seemed to be the muscle of their operation. Bill was tough and pretty big, as I recall, with a wispy beard. Besides that, I was outnumbered by the strippers as well! So I mean, look, I understood that. They had to make room for another project, so BookWars was starting to get phased out, or cut-only-at-night type of thing."

"Yes it was tough. I was not financially flush, didn't come from a rich family, had no connections...and moving around doesn't help, but I made the choice to move around the country in order to access the various editing systems I needed, and I was driven to make this movie. At the New Mexico screening, I'd seen the audience reaction to the rough assembly there on Superbowl Sunday, and seen that yes, it's taking shape, it's basically becoming a life form. So I felt driven and compelled to see it through to completion. All the way: For better or for worse, even though by the end I was just numb and wasted.

I had to push it through to completion, execution."

An uncertain period followed.

"So there was that phase in there, when the stripper union documentary came into the studio in San Francisco, and BookWars editing time was impacted and I wasn't living large. Work was sporadic and I had split up with my significant other in San Francisco, a woman from Argentina who I'd married during the process of making the movie. A lot was sort of seemingly in the air. That was the down point, where I nearly chucked it all in and took a midnight swim to Alcatraz. And Alcatraz was just down the street! I could see it night and day in the Bay. Taunting me, beckoning me."

"And then luckily, right after that–after that super-down point, I got the job at this start-up in San Francisco. It was an online directory of some kind, as I recall, that was in 1997 or 1998. I don't even know how they got my information. I sent out waves and waves of résumés throughout my time in San Francisco, of course, as I was continually looking for work to fund the project and to support myself. Anyway, this one hit, out of the blue, but they called me. Like start-ups do, they scoop in lots of people, and it was great. There were a lot of other young people working there–hundreds of others working this web indexing start-up. I was pretty satisfied, actually."

The filmmaker had reached a crossroads. A decision had to be made: head back to New York and finish the movie, leaving the comforts and stability of a new life behind? Or, stay and build up a new career, release the movie at its nearly completed state, or scrap it altogether? He elaborates:

"So, when the notion came up to come back to New York to finish the movie, to put the sword in it, it wasn't necessarily an easy decision. Because yes, I was still loyal to the project and New York City which I still loved–still loved the city. I've spent over ten years in New York, which makes me a New Yorker, at least according to Ed Koch! But, I was now enjoying some domestic comforts on the West coast...some regular salary for the first time in a long, long time. And this was like a drink of water in the middle of the desert. I mean, it's not romantic to move around from place to place without financial support, and trying to make it, and to bootstrap a project like this over the course of a couple years without a map or support, just using your wits and instincts. After a while, you get tired. It may sound fun and hippy-ish, but it's not really–it was at times a real grind and I wouldn't have done it if I didn't need to access the editing gear."

"I really did not necessarily feel like prying myself loose, but I was encouraged to come back to New York and finish it with the understanding that the movie would be pushed-completed, executed. That the involvement of a New York producer-Michel-would amplify its chances through his established connections...or so I thought. It didn't necessarily turn out that way. But those were the variables in the basket at the time, and I decided to go for it. And I was of course accountable for that choice, for better or worse."

How did he handle this at the new start-up?

"So, I quit the job at the start-up. Looking back on it, I'm not sure that was such a great move. Yet I was compelled by this utter obsession to complete the movie, while also under the belief that it would or could be sold more easily once I was back in New York and thus boost my career. So I saw it as an investment, though nothing was guaranteed. I try not to have regrets now as a matter of principle.... You've got to understand, the movie at that point was about 90% done. In other words, had I outputted to master format, it would have gotten into some movie festivals anyway at that point. It probably would have gotten some cable broadcasts. But that extra 10% may have made the difference between it being a world-class unique movie–which I think it is, even with its jazzy, grainy style–and a run of the mill indie documentary."

"But the question is: was it worth the sacrifice of livelihood? Because, I wasn't getting any financial support or grants. It was cheap Chinese food, every day, friend rice and so forth. I was applying like mad for grants, as I said. I would go down to the Foundation Center in San Francisco as often as I could. I researched foundations, applied there; I joined their organization, doing all this grant research. But the grants just didn't materialize. Not sure why, but it seems that the subject was not a blue chip grantable project, and I was, demographically speaking, not the ideal fundable demographic. I did get one grant, from the Playboy Foundation, actually–a thousand dollars. Not a lot of money but it boosted my morale."

I have to ask how the Playboy Foundation characterized the award.

"For the freedom-of-speech nature of BookWars!," Rosette replies."I enjoyed putting the Playboy bunny ears on my promotional materials afterwards, that was a bit of a gas. I felt like part of the Playboy family in a sly and subtle way. Anyway, prying myself loose from the West coast wasn't easy after finally getting a decent job and settling in to some comforts...I had a new girlfriend, I was working at the start-up with a lot of fun, cool people. I was finally comfortable. It was really, really tough to pull myself out of that and go back to New York to finish the movie. I was tired, you know? I was tired, but...I followed the advice I received from the industry and from Michel, and from others, and my own senses. I made the decision–I'm accountable for the choice anyway, even if the potential outcome was romanticized or idealized. I went back."

Given the constant work and stress, didn't the idea of packing and driving cross country feel nearly overwhelming?

"I didn't drive back. I was...as you probably could understand, I was at that point still quite burned out and couldn't face another cross-country drive. I flew back with, I think, trying to remember, I think I flew back with all the tapes. No. I flew back and shipped all the boxes back. I shipped all the tapes back, and all my other stuff–sweaters and things hidden inside. That's right. You know the old trick: you say it's Media Mail and get a discount.

Most of it was media, true, but the Postal Service was pretty lax back then and didn't check, just took your word for it. But now they're really strict. I tried to do that recently again in Los Angeles, when I was back in the States but no, they're very strict about sending stuff at Media Rate now. Back then I sent everything I had accumulated in San Francisco hidden in and amongst the master tapes from the editing process. Boxes and boxes. And they arrived in Michel's office in New York. And I carried on, I continued editing."

Morale had to be in short supply. How did Rosette sustain it?

"How did I sustain my own morale? The toughest part, the deepest dips in morale, were not happening in the final stretch in New York. The deepest dip in morale for me was happening at that crucial moment, right before I'd gotten the job at the start-up in San Francisco, when my finances were in shambles, the movie was about 90% complete, but still not totally finished. I was living in a residential hotel–or was I at that point? No. I was living in the apartment that I'd shared with my wife at the time from Argentina, before we split up. That was before I got the job at the start-up. I didn't have a lot of money."

"One of the reasons we split up is that the woman I was with, this artist I was with–we were married at the time–she couldn't understand that I was editing so much at night. She was convinced I was having some kind of affair. But I was editing: across town, on the edge of Chinatown...editing BookWars."

"And she was...because she's from Argentina she was convinced I was having an affair, seeing another woman. That's what she explained later, that's what she thought, based on the cultural behavior she was familiar with down in South America. And that drove a wedge between us. Plus, all my money was going toward the movie. It wasn't true, by the way–I was editing. But she couldn't conceive of the fact that I was actually grinding away until 11 or 12 o'clock at night on a movie, and then coming back across town to the Upper Haight from North Beach on this beat-up scooter I'd bought for $200 at an auction. But it's true. I was loyal."

With some trepidation, I ask if money (lack of) was a factor.

"I think so. As mentioned, I didn't have a lot of extra cash. All the money was going into tapes and supplies, and sustaining–you know–the edit, and I couldn't buy a lot of comforts. I know this may sound sexist or whatever to some, but I couldn't buy a lot of the 'nest' items that are essential to keep relationships happy. I mean, it's one thing to live, you know, in an edgy style on one's own. Anyone can grit their teeth and bear it for themselves. But when you're in a relationship or–more expansively–a family situation, then you need more in the nest. And I wasn't able to provide that, because of every shred of...I had to finish this movie. And I was trying to make a nest, but I just couldn't reach that level at that time. And who knows? Maybe it's for the better in the big picture of the universe. But that was the toughest time."

"And so, how did I sustain my own morale during that time? I would call my friends–Rich, who is a musician. He did the music for BookWars...the slide guitar stuff. Actually we met on the way to a catering job...I was working as a caterer. You know, just serving people plates of hors d'oeuvres and shit. Making some extra bucks. And there was a guy, another catering guy going to the same gig, and it was too far to ride on my scooter so I said 'hey, can I have a ride?' And we met up and it turned out it was Rich, Rich Goldstein, this musician also known as Little Muddy on the West Coast. Cool guy, talented musician, and we're still in touch. And we hit it off. We're talking, on the way to the job, and I mentioned that I was putting the movie together and he ended up doing the intro music for BookWars. The slide guitar sections, not the jazz stuff in the middle, which was the work of two great jazz legends, Willis Jackson and Jack McDuff."

"But, when in my deepest, 'downest' moments, I would call Rich, aka Muddy. Or another friend in the arts who could understand the situation. Someone who could relate, who was not...you know, there's two strata of artists really, or creative people. There are those who are coming from established families, you know, sort of patrician families who may have a lot of backing or funding from their lineage. Or they have their long-time families in the area with various existing assets and connections which they can draw upon to make the process easier."

"Then, there are those creatives–and I was in the latter category–who hammer away and claw away to get by without much subsidy. Not that we don't try to be subsidized...I just think a lot of it comes down to having existing family connections and assets, or not. The artistic drive isn't absent: just the backing, connections, and assets. It sounds reductionist, maybe, but I think we all know this is true to some degree, especially in America today and in the previous decade or so."

"And so this was the case with Rich, and myself. And I guess, you know, he could understand the struggle I was going through, and so I contacted him. Michel also, you know, he put in some good words–uplifting words, advice, during that time. But he was farther away; he was back in New York."

"So that time was the deepest darkest time, the Pit. Right after the stripper Union movie came to the studio and I had to scale down BookWars, but before I had the new girlfriend and job at the tech startup. The future of the movie was uncertain. I still was working sporadic odd jobs–trying to get full-time work before I landed the job at the start-up. And during that time, during that pit, perhaps as a result of the stress, I split up with my wife at the time."

With so much turbulence in his personal and professional life at that time, the filmmaker must have thought once or twice about that 'midnight swim to Alcatraz'. But what pulled him up again in the morning?

"What pulled me up in the morning? I don't know. To answer your question, I think it's more like...you need to just try to shut off that part of your mind that feels pain.

That part that feels doubt. Turn it off. Physically push any thoughts out of your head that don't support your survival and mission. Don't look back; don't think. It's like you have to force your mind to shut off thoughts about the future or the past, if you're in that situation. That's what I did at least. And just focus on plowing ahead any way you can. Clawing away, moving forward."

"And then something eventually, hopefully, will break. And for me, it was getting the job at the start-up, which in turn precipitated, you know, a better standard of living. I was making better money, I met a really cool girlfriend while I was working at the start-up, and everything was working well. And then the call came that the studio in New York was opened up. They offered to let me come there and use it to finish the movie–not for free, I would still have to pay, but it could be deferred–and that was one of those 'Life Crossroad choices': Do I go back and finish it? Or, because the movie is about 90% done, do I just call it a day and say it's finished? As it is–without pushing it the extra 10%, without giving it everything? Which may in turn enable the movie to achieve a higher, more rarified standard. Which in turn could lead to a moviemaking career breakthrough. It was a tough choice, really."

"If I'd stayed in San Francisco, comfortably working at

the start-up, and mind you it was quite comfortable...and others who continued to work there, others from my cohort, went on to get stock options! Not just options–they'd actually sold those stocks after they matured. One of them bought a houseboat in Sausalito, things like that. But I felt this inner imperative: I gotta' give it the best shot I can. If I leave the movie now, well, on one hand I will know I didn't give it 100%. On the other hand, there was also conjectural-type data which I thought were based on my conversations with Michel, the New York co-producer. That my coming to New York and finishing it there would parlay into better connections in the local industry there, and a better probability of the movie getting exposure and distribution."

With Negroponte waiting, the prospects of becoming a documentarian must have been fairly thrilling. Was this an end goal?

"I wasn't necessarily seeking to become a documentary filmmaker. Yet BookWars was a documentary. I don't actually see much difference between fiction and documentary–it's all storytelling to me, and it's all subjective anyway. I've also made fiction movies, with storyboarding, coverage, continuity, matching action, and so forth, so I would say that fiction is technically more challenging to produce than documentaries. But they both exist on the same storytelling spectrum. Anyway there was this discussion, and understanding that the movie would–with Michel onboard as a co-producer–would be pushed more vigorously, and would probably become sold and exhibited more widely than it would if I was doing it on my own from San Francisco. No guarantees, obviously, but taking that entire basket, that entire formula, and trusting my colleagues, I opted to head back to New York to execute the movie as best I could."

Was filming among the booksellers particularly challenging, with the mix of personalities?

"The actual shooting of the movie at the bookstands was not a problem," says Rosette. "The booksellers knew me already for a couple of years. It wasn't like, 'Oh, here's this documentary filmmaker coming.' It was, 'Oh, here's Jason with a camera.' I was like a guy making home movies–that's what it was. It wasn't tough at all to shoot on West 4th Street, and Astor Place and Third Avenue where I had also set up. Shooting on Sixth Avenue...well, I didn't sell on Sixth Avenue. It was a different scene, as you can see in the movie. But, even then, the guys on Sixth Avenue, they sort of knew who was selling on West 4th, because there was some crossover in the scene."

"In other words, if you were a bookseller you knew about the different clusters, the different areas. And so, when I went and introduced myself on Sixth Avenue, even then I wasn't a total stranger because I was an actual bookseller, just selling in a different area. And we could talk. I could 'talk the Talk'. And they could come and stop by West 4th, or Third Avenue when I was actually selling books, and see for themselves, that I was actually out there as well, slinging books for a living. So, I was part of the overall herd, or the tribe."

2. WORKING IN THE PUBLIC FORUM: RECOLLECTIONS

BookWars follows a surprisingly clear, linear path, and viewers get a beginning-to-end sense of journalistic narrative, with no background hint of the filmmaker's far-flung travels around the country in search of equipment. Rosette had worked for nearly four years on the street in New York City as a self-employed sidewalk bookseller, hunting for books, dealing with the elements, the people of the city, and more. I wondered: aside from the making of the movie, were there any really low points during the bookselling itself, when he thought forget it, this is too much...weather, fatigue, police hassles...?

Rosette's low, deadpan voice doesn't hesitate."Yeah, there were some great times out there. But there were some low points, too –a lot of low points. I mean: we were bootstrapping a living, making a living with an unregistered microenterprise, a small business right there on the sidewalks of New York City. So, it was at its core a business, a mini-startup. Let's say you're having a slow day, and you're not making any sales. I would sometimes think, well, I'm still trying to get freelance work and I'm still trying to finish my first movie Charlie's Box, so I need to make more money to put toward that, but there are no sales, so then along comes the horrific doubt. The doubt that I will ever finish this movie, a movie I was working on at the time, called Charlie's Box."

"You know, when you're standing there out on the street, and the wind is blowing and you're not making sales, maybe there isn't another bookseller near you so you're kind of just standing there on your own, watching the world go by. Those are moments where you may deflate. When the sales aren't happening, the books seem to be almost like a curse. So, yes, there were many times when I thought, 'oh-forget it'. And that was of course the final moment in the movie, BookWars, which is essentially recreated based on that feeling from those times. You know, there were many times when I wanted to say 'fuck it,' and I wanted to be ideally, you know, hired as a director making films. I mean I had graduated from NYU Film School, a Trustee Scholar, and was doing everything

I could to make movies and get ahead as best I could."

"When you know your skills and capabilities but you're frustrated and unable to get satisfaction, to exercise those skills and capabilities, yes, that can be frustrating. Selling books in and of itself is not an art form, you know. It's an interesting occupation, but it's not the same as writing a book, or writing a great novel, you know. So, in a way, I guess during those moments of doubt, looking at a table full of books–great works–thinking, my god, these people, these men, these women, these photographers, these painters, they all were able to exercise their form of expression. And me, I'm standing here, I feel like a leaf in an eddy behind a waterfall."

I have to admit kinship. As a novelist, primarily, I've frequently felt like that spinning leaf. I realized at that moment that this is a universal point of what the filmmaker was sharing, something that folks in almost any field could relate to at some time or another. Rosette continues:

"On the other hand, at other times it felt great to be out there, absolutely superb, as you see in the movie. Feeling the beat and pulse of the city, at the table–it was was a real node. So there were ups as well as downs. The police were less than a hassle for us over on West 4th street, but they came by more frequently during the [then-Mayor] Giuliani times, and they started ramping things up. Hassling a bit more, enforcing the one-table-per-person standard, enforcing the distance between planters. The university over on West 4th had put these giant planters out to try to stop booksellers from setting up there."

"These things sort of chip away, and they say to you, well, you are not an official person. You are not a valued member of society. Nobody is coming out saying 'we appreciate your being here' except for the customers. The customers would come and say-'God, you guys are great! Wow, I'm so glad I found you guys.' You know, that sort of thing. So the people clearly expressed it, but the establishment–the powers that be–extending all the way up to the epic real estate level, and the level of the administration of the city...I didn't discern that the role of the sidewalk booksellers were an appreciated thing in the official society. It was just a 'You are people on the street. You must follow this law,' sort of thing. It had nothing to do with books, from their point of view."

"So to answer your question: fatigue, and the feeling of isolation, sometimes were the main antagonists in the life of the sidewalk bookseller, at least as I experienced it. Hassles by the cops and other powers of the city came second. Now that formula might be inverted for the booksellers on Sixth Avenue, who were hassled by the Sixth Precinct far more frequently and vigorously. Sidewalk bookselling was a unique job. In fact it was so unique that, besides your cohorts, there weren't many people who necessarily related to the actual experience of doing it. Not just standing there and selling the books, that's the easy part–[but] going out and getting the books. Hunting for them. Storing them. Repairing them. Hitting the road to find them–the hunt...all that and more."

3. (FILM) SCHOOL OF HARD KNOCKS

Rosette attended film school, something about which aspiring filmmakers seem endlessly curious, and besiege working directors with is-it-worth-it? type queries. Most advise these questioners simply to get outside and start learning by doing. What is Rosette's take on this?

"I would agree," he replies. "I learned most of my skills from actually doing. And I would say that is the way of the bootstrapper, at heart, whatever the field. My first movie Charlie's Box–a drama. I wore a lot of hats. I scripted it, story-boarded it, produced it, hired the crew, sourced the gear. I did that on my own, after graduating from NYU Film School. It was my first independent film. And working on films, working on movies, you know, as a PA [production assistant] or a runner or a location coordinator, whatever. That's all hands-on. Making

BookWars was also completely learning-by-doing. Making my second feature, Lost in New Mexico, again, it was learning by doing, with some research and networking to fill in the gaps."

"Without any scholarships or loans, I would say, you know, I wouldn't have gone to NYU–it's very expensive. I had about half of it paid for by scholarships, and then I also worked as a caddie when I was a teenager in Ohio. I had a caddie scholarship and some other weird scholarship, I forget now. It was like...some religious group...I forget now. But I had a conglomeration of different grants and scholarships that paid for about half my tuition at NYU."

Lacking these monies, would he have found some way to attend?

"Had that not occurred, I would not have gone there. And perhaps that would have been better; maybe that would have been the better route. It's very popular, you know, a lot of filmmakers are asked these questions. A lot of movie people are asked these questions, and often they'll be diplomatic and so forth and I'll try to be. But, I also have to be honest and say that given the expense of attending–even with the scholarship, and the fact that, although I had some good professors there–the school kind of dropped the ball in terms of seeing what was ahead, technologically speaking–in terms of bringing non-linear editing into the school at the very cusp of that technology–and making that available to us. I mean, we were still editing on tape-to-tape systems in the undergrad program around the time Avid was released."

"I would say, any top-notch cutting-edge institution, in any field, should be on the ball regarding the cutting edge developments, and should be giving its students the first looks and hands-on experience with those industry developments. And that wasn't happening, at least for the undergrad program. So to answer the question, I would say it was mixed. I know this is an unpopular or unfashionable thing to say, that you're supposed to be totally, gushingly supportive of your Alma Mater no matter what or else you'll be branded a 'bad guy.' Perhaps you'll be banished to some degree. But I feel the need to be objective in order to assist those who are coming along and making the same decisions I did–tried to make–when I was seventeen."

"Believe it or not, I've mentioned this before and then heard folks had shown up in Asia, where I am now, asking around saying 'Hey, where's the guy that hates NYU?' I know, it's amazing, but it's true. I heard about this first-hand though from the Dean of Media studies at a university in Cambodia where I had been working at the time. Anyway, for the record, let's make this official: I don't hate NYU. That's ridiculous. I mean, the Alumni office contacted me recently where I was working at the US Embassy in Yangon [Rangoon]. I was a teacher in the Public Affairs department at the American Center. I'd been fully vetted by the State Department and was in fact an employee of the State Department, though my main task was youth-centered teaching. Anyway, NYU seemed cordial enough–they were seeking a donation from me, ironically. God bless 'em, have to admire their reach. I say ironically because I'm still paying off my student loans and debts for my movies! So, no, of course, I don't 'hate' NYU, that's absurd. Even with all the unwelcome behavior they demonstrated towards the street booksellers on West 4th street. But I have to relate my experience from attending film school there as objectively as possible for those who may be considering sustaining that cost."

"Now, I wouldn't say going to film school was a complete loss either. It was a mixed experience, as most things are. There were a couple of great teachers there actually. One of them was an acting teacher and, in fact, that's how I got turned on to acting. It was through the Actors' Craft, one of these classes we took during the undergrad film program, that I met the late, great Marketa Kimbrell–a lot of people who know her, or who read or hear this, will know who I'm talking about. She was a great drama teacher. She was in that movie The Pawnbroker [1965 drama directed by Sidney Lumet] by the way, the original Pawnbroker. I had a transformative experience in that class, it was great, and it directly led to my interest in continuing to act on stage and on-camera whenever I could. So how can you put a monetary value on that? I probably wouldn't have met her, or had that experience if I had not gone to NYU. So in that sense, yeah, it was worth it."

"Another great teacher I had, who passed away recently–Milek Knebel from Israel–he was very strict but nice, goodhearted. Not really a millimeter of bullshit in him when it came to critiquing students' work, and he would really tell you what he felt, and I appreciate that. I would call him a great teacher too. So there were at least two great teachers I met there."

"So, was it worth it? Here's what I think now. I've looked back on this question a lot, and what I would say to someone considering attending film school or any form of other higher education would be: try to look at it as an investment. Don't undertake it as speculation, such as 'hey, if I attend so-and-so school, I'm likely to get work doing so-and-so within this period of time.' Don't use 'likelihood' as a way to justify the expense. You must determine a definite linkage between the investment in attending and your increased quality of life and livelihood afterwards. If you can't identify an absolutely solid, verifiable linkage–then forget about it. Ask yourself, 'what is the guarantee that I will be able to recover or recoup that that tuition money, and how quickly will I do so, after I graduate?'"

Was the more practical, business side of the art addressed?

"The business sensibility was not significantly present at NYU, at least in the undergraduate program. NYU Film, undergrad, was more of an art school. And this is literally the case: NYU Film is part of Tisch School of the Arts. I think more of the business side would have been welcome though; you know, how to market your completed movie, how to create a one-sheet, how to find broadcasters and buyers, etc. How to make a living while working towards larger and more distant industry goals. It took me a while to develop those bootstrapping skills on my own, you know, after I graduated. I really had to develop the business sensibility on my own. It took me...well, even during the BookWars years I didn't have the full-blown business sensibility that I needed, which I have cultivated somewhat since then. But during the release of that movie, and the making of earlier projects, I had no clue."

"Our professors were saying things like, 'hey, just go fund your movie using credit cards!' Now, granted, this approach was back in the late 80's and 90's, when that was all the rage. But it's a risky and terribly moronic approach. I went ahead and did just that when funding my first indie project, Charlie's Box, and I still haven't recouped that. My car had broken down at the time and the bank instructed the tow truck driver to take my credit card, actually-I'd overextended myself making that movie and had trouble paying it off. But I'm accountable, even if I was clueless myself and listening to clueless advisors. It was my choice. In any case, I'm now, belatedly, a lot more in tune with the business sensibility of spending money on producing media."

"On the other hand, one significantly positive aspect of film school is that you do make contacts who you will maintain for a while. I'm still in touch with a fair number of colleagues from my NYU days. You know, it's really hard to quantify it...'is it worth x-amount of dollars.' You have to sit down with a pad of paper, spreadsheet-whatever...and make, you know, make a list. The pluses, the minuses...can you afford it? What is the verifiable, projected payoff?""

"Hey, here's another one. It also has to do with how much of an impact–if at all–a negative financial impact will it have on you to attend. Let's say you attend; you go to a fairly expensive school. If you're subsidized, either through a grant or a rich family, whatever, and it...let's say in the worse-case scenario it's a washout: what would be the financial impact? If the financial impact of that worse-case scenario is negligible, then go ahead. However, if you're going to an expensive school and you're not subsidized, either through rich family or grants or scholarships, I would think twice. I'd be very careful of student loans, by the way. Jeez...that's another subject. I've paid off on a great deal of mine, but still have a few even at this age, years later. All from a decision I made to take out student loans nearly 30 years ago."

What if one knows the financial impact will be negative. Is the learning aspect worth it?

"If the impact is going to be extremely negative, or if there's not a strong guarantee that you will either A) recoup you investment in your education in a reasonable amount of time, or B) in the event of a washout, have negligible financial repercussions, then I would say avoid it. Go to a school that's less expensive. Or don't go to university, go to a trade school or just start bootstrapping it learning 'hands-on' any way you can."

4. FERLINGHETTI'S ANARCHIST / GUERILLA SHOOTING IN NYC

I was curious–perhaps overly so–about how Rosette supported himself during the New York shoot of his first feature, BookWars, the movie which had compelled me to make contact with him. Did he pick up any freelance gigs, or was bookselling paying rent, buying film stock, covering processing, etc.? His voice rises from the speaker:

"Well, you know, BookWars was shot mainly on video, with some Super 8 film, and a lot of that had to do with the cameras that were available. In the beginning I was borrowing equipment, bootstrapping everything. I didn't have my own equipment–I didn't have any money. I was getting by with rent, but was not in a position to fund a motion picture project according to any normal standard.

Yet, I was compelled to make this movie. Tried for grants but didn't have any luck, and I didn't feel like waiting around for those to come through in order to start shooting. When a video camera, of any format, materialized, I used that. Similarly, when a Super 8 camera became available I used that. And film stock for Super 8 is pretty cheap, but not as cheap as video of course. It was about fourteen dollars for Tri-X black and white, and the processing was like twenty two dollars for something like that. Color was like sixteen dollars, plus twenty seven or thirty for processing; I forget now. So obviously Super 8 had to be shot more sparingly. Most of the shooting was done on video."

"And it was not a single shoot. It was an ongoing–as is the case with most documentaries–it was an ongoing process that went on for quite a while. Shooting here and there...picking up shots, editing, picking up more shots, shooting some more. So the shoot extended–'shoot' quote unquote–technically extended from 1995 until 1999...no, even 2000. Because the movie was finished and released in June 2000. It went to the New York Underground Film Festival in March, and it was still a fine cut, and I think I was still doing a little shooting in the beginning of 2000. So, a five-year shoot. But not straight through."

I mention that claims along these lines—"chronicled over 10 years!"—pervade our culture.

Addressing this, Rosette says, "It's kind of a curiosity that you'll see. I would suggest people use their critical thinking in those situations. That is, whenever you encounter a project, a film or a research project, sociology textbook, whatnot, where the author says, you know, 'made over the course of 20 years!'—you know that's a kind of selling point. But that doesn't necessarily mean that they spent 20 straight years making it, most likely. It means that they did some shooting or writing or researching at one point, and then paused, and then went back to it at another point. So the aggregate amount may only have been a year, or six actual months of shooting, or writing in the case of a book."

"So it's a curious thing, when people use that technique as a selling point.'Made over the course of 10 years!' or '20 years in the making!' Let's say you picked up the camera for an hour in Year One, and then five years later you went back and picked it up for an afternoon. You can't very well say that that's five years of work. But you know how it is. People want sensational things to consume and to sell and market and, you know, god bless 'em. But for anyone who's hearing that as, like, a selling point, whether it is a movie or a novel or a sociological textbook, I would suggest taking that with a grain of salt. On the other hand, BookWars was in fact made over the course of five years–that's verifiable."

Getting back to the shooting and production of the movie, I wondered if the filmmaker had picked up any freelance gigs, or was bookselling covering all costs–paying rent, buying film and video stock, covering processing, etc.

"Did I pick up freelance gigs? Yeah, there were plenty of other gigs I did during the bookselling days. Bookselling was like an alternate, meat-and-potatoes type micro-enterprise. It was a micro-enterprise, which required little up-front overhead, except time, effort, and an ability to hunt for books. Yet, it also generated cash. Those were the appealing aspects of it. It wasn't like a dream job completely; there was a lot of hard work involved. But it was appealing in that the overhead was low and it filled the gaps."

I comment that it looked very interesting, at least from what I'd seen in the movie, having this unusual occupation out in the public form of such a massive American city.

"It was. It was a unique and fairly interesting job; I mean, you're dealing with books and not just like, you know, knock-off handbags from China. And, you know, this means that when there's some down-time you can actually poke through some books and read them. So street bookselling was like a...it was one of a palette of different occupations I had at the time. At times it was full-time. And sometimes–by the nature of it–you could pack it up and put it into storage. Let's say, for example, I had a freelance gig for a week, or five days. I would go and do the gig. I would put the books aside and just stick them in storage, and go and do the gig. Bring the books out again when the gig was over."

"But who can say whether that's the most successful approach or not? To have a parallel job as a financial hedge? Maybe psychologically it's best to commit yourself to only doing one thing, your ideal target job, and to say 'I'm only going to look for freelance film gigs and nothing else, because then my mind will force me to find the gigs,' etc. You know that train of thought. However, I think it's wise to reduce one's exposure in a variable economy by having multiple revenue streams, which is what I found when I emerged from NYU in the early 90s. And so, that's basically what bookselling was as a financial thing."

"But as mentioned, the movie was completely self-funded. Except for an advance I got near the very end from ARTE/ZDF, a French-German broadcaster. They gave an advance based on a contract I'd signed for the hour-long broadcast rights in Europe–the TV premiere of the movie in Europe. So I used that advance as finishing money, as well as a way to pay off some of my debts, including some student loans. That was at the very, very end. But the entire rest of the process was completely self-funded. No fundraising from the producers, either, although the Montoyas let me use their equipment on a deferred basis. I'm still paying it off, actually, even to this day. But there was no fundraising; there was no crowd-sourcing. None of the actual producers involved were actual, fundraising producers in that sense."

How did Rosette handle those occasions when, selling books at his table and shooting, more supplies were needed to continue production?

"If it came time to buy some film or video stock–if I was out of raw stock and I wanted to pick up some shots, if it was a nice day, and there was an interesting vibe...or good lighting. Let's say it was film. Well, I'd ask somebody to watch the table, and I would run over to Rafik on Broadway. Rafik was a film and video supply house upstairs in this loft on Broadway. Not sure if it's still there; all the old-time New York indie filmmakers must remember Rafik. Great place. I remember their slanted old stairway, going upstairs into the strange upper loft where they did business. It was like something out of The Cabinet of Dr. Caligari."

"Anyway, I'd run up there and get a couple rolls of Super 8, come back downstairs and shoot. Or, run to one of the pharmacies that had Hi 8 or Regular 8 video tape. I think I was shooting on Hi 8 sometimes, and Regular 8 at other times...and Super VHS too! It depended, you know, [on] the camera I had lying around. Because I didn't have funds to buy a camera; I was borrowing. So yes, as the books were sold, I would have a wad of cash there and finally go and buy more stock or video, and then just keep going. It was pure bootstrapping. That's how it worked when I was in New York."

Were the same methods used in San Francisco?

"When I was editing the movie in San Francisco it was different, because I couldn't sell books–they didn't have a street bookselling scene. I looked into it. There was no used bookselling scene on the street in San Francisco–I was a bit surprised. I mean, there's a very happening literary scene there of course. City Lights Bookstore, the Beats, Lawrence Ferlinghetti.... I met up with Ferlinghetti briefly, by the way, and I gave him a tape of the cut in progress. He liked it. He said it was 'anarchistic.' I'm not sure I agree completely with his assessment, but it was great to get his reaction. And he's, you know, one of the last of the Beats-one of the last original Beats. His shop, City Lights Bookstore, was where I made contact with him. Anyway, aside from the literary tradition of San Francisco, there was not a street bookselling scene. I couldn't do the books, so I did other odd jobs in San Francisco."

"I was a bicycle cab driver, for tourists and others down in Chinatown, Fisherman's Wharf...that's a whole other story. Jeez-what a job that was. Very physical. I was in pretty good shape, had once ridden from Colorado to San Francisco solo by bicycle, through the Southwest, then continuing on through the desert and up the coast to San Francisco. That's another story. But as mentioned, there were some seriously challenging rides at times as a bicycle cab driver. I took a massive Samoan couple with their huge cooler of beer on my first day. Waiters from nearby restaurants on Pacific Street stepped outside to marvel at my creaking, groaning progress up the hill with that six hundred pound load: just my poor legs and some Chinatown dim sum pulling it all."

"What else? I was a temp, doing office admin work. Sometimes it was very chill and easy–and sometimes it was boring and empty. But it paid the bills–whatever it takes. I did editing gigs when I could find them, and worked on a few movies that way. Whatever I needed to do to keep going, I would do. I had to. I tried, even while I was applying for grants, researching grants down at the Foundation Center."

"But, as I said, I wasn't able to get much action with the grants. BookWars was not a grantable project, really, I think in retrospect it was...well, it fell between the cracks of the fundable demographics, you know. So I had to bootstrap it.

I had to fund it myself, out of pocket. Live by your wits and do whatever it takes to keep going. That is the heart of bootstrapping it."

5. THE CAMERA EYE / FILM & DIGITAL

A lot has changed, technologically and culturally, since BookWars. In today's digital environment, even with the democratization of the field since the late 90s with inexpensive desktop editing and DSLR shooting gear, there are directors who still prefer the smell of acetate. Undoubtedly, film stock has an evocative texture lacking in digital. I wondered what Rosette's take was on this matter, since his documentary employs both traditional film and video.

"The short answer is, it depends on the budget. And, actually, what genre you're working in. In documentary, it's just prohibitive, really, to be shooting on film. Shooting so much material–often like a 50: 1 or 100: 1 ratio, it's just not cost-effective to shoot on film, generally speaking. And that's what BookWars was shot on–mainly video. But as you can see, in the movie I shot some material on film, which I used as sort of poetic interlude material between beats or chapters. I couldn't shoot the entire movie on film, but I wanted to have some of the–as you said–evocative texture of film. The molecular structure of film, and its dye molecules suspended in an emulsion. A filmic base...a physical base."

"It's analog. The molecules of dye suspended in a film emulsion are–by their very nature–randomly oriented to some degree. Whereas digital is digital and mechanical at the nano-level; it's ones and zeroes lined up in a mechanical fashion on a sensor. And you also have certain organic anomalies in film stock that you would not find in digital. Sometimes, even though it may be well-produced film stock according to very strict specifications, you might have certain areas where there's some micro-anomaly with the dye suspended in a more concentrated fashion, and it creates an organic grain structure."

I ask if cost is a factor.

"The challenge," Rosette answers, "is that film is expensive to shoot. You can't, you know, re-record over it, and it's expensive to process. So for an indie project like BookWars, it would have been prohibitive to shoot on film. It depends on the genre and project though. If you're shooting fiction, a narrative project which has been really strictly storyboarded out, and your shooting ratio is lower, like 20: 1–something like that–or even 10: 1, then film becomes a viable option. Like the movie I'd made before BookWars, Charlie's Box–that was shot entirely on 16mm. That was doable because I had carefully storyboarded and covered it; it was a drama, after all and it thus didn't require the shooting ratios of a typical documentary."

"Moving even further up the ladder: if you have a big-budget film with name talent involved, then, when breaking down the entire budget of the project, you'll see that the cost of film stock then becomes just a fractional, almost marginal, expense compared to the other costs. The talent, production costs, crew, etc. So film stock and processing, when you get into the bigger-budget movies with name talent involved, well, it's the talent fees which are huge in that case. And the cost of film stock, processing, and even the digital scanning or telecine is just a thin layer on the cake."

"In that sense, if the budget is high, and you've got name talent involved, and if you're shooting, say, a fiction film, a narrative movie which is planned, shot and storyboarded...then acquisition on film is a viable option. It is viable, and many movies are still shot on film at that level. When you get down to the indie-level films, though, where there's not name talent involved or it's like a SAG [Screen Actors Guild] low-budget agreement level, or something like that, then the cost of film stock starts to become prohibitive in terms of the payoff you get versus the 'look and feel.'"

"And the digital ecosystem is enormous of course and is here to stay until some yet-to-be-imagined future technology replaces it– whatever that may be. There are new generations of Arriflex, digital cameras, the Red cameras...and you know, there's the DSLR for low-budget movies. DSLR cameras are completely ubiquitous now. So you can get, let's say, a Canon Rebel for six-hundred dollars with a kit lens, and you can actually shoot something with that. It's not necessarily the best quality; the APS sensor is smaller on those cameras. But let's say you step up to a full-frame DSLR, say the Sony a7 series, the body maybe costs $2200, and you can have–or even rent, depending on where you are–prime lenses or high end lenses to go with that, and shoot 4K and get some really good looking imagery."

So budget really is a much larger factor than I had assumed. What if a filmmaker has a substantial amount to work with?

"Let's say, if money was not an issue, and it just came down to convenience. Well, digital is more convenient in most ways as well, because when you acquire the image, if you're acquiring in digital then you can load it onto your machine directly from the card or drive. If you're shooting on film, it needs to be scanned. Scanned-in or telecined, and then loaded from the telecine or scan format. So that process alone hints at a bigger-budget movie."

I wonder if the filmmaker employs a particular system and method these days, or is that dependent on the scope of a given film, and how he plans on telling its story?

"I'm not particularly attached to either [digital or film] in terms of an ideology.", Rosette says. "As you can discern from this discussion, I would shoot with whatever is available, the best medium that's available that can drive the story and project. Film...digital...it doesn't matter to me. The best I can get, whatever that may be."

"You know, there's a big wave in the industry, many people working to save and preserve film stock as an acquisition medium, for artistic, cultural and historical purposes. Now, I think they're motivated not only by the unique texture and capture quality of film, but also for the nostalgia of film. That is, the sentiment, versus an overriding practical impetus. But I look at it this way: what if by some chance, video had been invented before film, which is of course not true, film has been around a lot longer. But what if it were the reverse? Would people be sentimental and nostalgic about video, if film was supplanting video?"

"I know, for instance, some media and filmmakers who are nostalgic about the 'look' of early video, which is gone now. The black and white early video with the strange, crisp black halo around everything. Technically, it's a mess, but there are folks who are nostalgic about that. In other words, I think there's an element of romanticism and sentiment involved as well, in the trend to save and preserve shooting on film for film's sake."

"No doubt, it does have a different look. However, if you don't have the budget to shoot on film, then if you–as a producer or filmmaker–are stretching and breaking the bank to shoot on film, you would probably be better served to shoot on a high-resolution digital format instead. And thereby gain flexibility in post-production and acquisition of the images, and so forth. So my short response is, yeah, film looks great. But I'm not particularly attached. Whatever best serves the project and the team behind the project."

Aside from limitations of budget, what format might best serve a looser, more improvised project?

"If you have an improvisational kind of movie," Rosette says, "then certainly video would likely be better. Something like Shadows, movies of the style Cassavetes produced...I strongly imagine that he would be shooting on digital now if he were around today. Of course, the Dogme 95 filmmakers and their successors have been shooting on small-format video for the same reason. But, if you have a movie that is really, clearly, and carefully storyboarded and covered in a classical fashion, then you probably could go for film. And if you have a massive budget with name talent involved, then it's a non-issue. You can do whatever you like. The cost of film stock and processing at that point, at those budget levels, becomes a marginal cost. It also depends on the kind of film. There's a trend toward shooting super fine-grained film stock...super fine-grained film stock, even in the high ISOs, so you can hardly see the grain. And, to me at least, you can hardly see a difference between that and a high-resolution digital format."

"So in that instance, if you're intent on shooting really fine-grained material...or if the script or story calls for a fine-grained look–like a romantic comedy, which doesn't really want grain. They want really crisp, clear, sharp, grainless images. But if you're shooting a grittier project, then the grain of film might harmonize better with your story."

I ask what type of film stock he used during most of BookWars' shoot.

"Well, for BookWars, since it was–since it is–a gritty street-driven project, I wanted to have the grainiest, grittiest looking film I could. And of course, my budget was a bare-ass minimum, as mentioned. So naturally I turned toward Super 8, which has such a small frame size that the blobs of dye, the dye crystals in the emulsion, are relatively large."

"And that's what gives the Super 8 its look, its grainy dancing look, which worked perfectly for the kind of story I was telling with BookWars: the streets of New York needed something very gritty, jazzy, with a sort of classic, archival dancing character. The Super 8 was woven in mainly as interludes or chapter breaks between 'beats' or scenes in the unfolding story."

6. SUPER 8 ARCHAEOLOGY / BOOKS & THE BOATHOUSE

Jason Rosette's love of books is evident, and he acknowledges in BookWars' end-credits Emily Dickinson, Rimbaud, Céline, Burroughs, Kerouac, Dylan Thomas, and others–potent dreamers all, who were beyond "passionate" (that much-vandalized, New Normal term) about books, and whose work is as relevant and fierce today as ever. BookWars in fact was praised by legendary poet/publisher Lawrence Ferlinghetti. Obvious in the film is that many, if not all, of Rosette's fellow booksellers also loved books and reading. Pete Whitney definitely earned his title as King of the Booksellers. Did love of books lead Rosette to cinematic storytelling, or vice-versa?

"That is an interesting question," he says. "I think it was simultaneous–my love of books and my engagement with movies. I remember, at about age 10 or 12 or thereabouts, always having some book lying around. It didn't really matter what the book was, it could be the World Book Encyclopedia-I just liked having words around. I would read at night until I would fall asleep, and then just leave it lying there in the bed. I liked to have books lying around in the bed with me, like a cat or pet, as I recall."

"And I liked reading, even back then. However, the movie thing's interesting I guess because it came from a link with my father, who died when I was eight. That left a big hole, you know, in my life. My brother was four years younger, so he was somehow less impacted I think. He says he tended to remember our father as a sort of mythical Obi Wan figure, hazy, shrouded in memory. But for me, I was eight, so I was more conscious of my father and his passing away."

"Now, the thing is, my father was a brilliant physicist, working on very rarified, arcane levels with crystal technology. He had developed new technologies, certain types of crystals that were used as laser windows they were attempting to use to trigger controlled fusion reactions. High level stuff like that, some of it very classified. He had patents and everything...but he died young, when he was 43. Aside from physics, he was also into fishing, photography-and movies. And he had a movie camera-a Super 8 camera. He was always shooting Super 8 films when I was growing up. That was his thing. We watched movies, Super 8 films, all the time. So, sometime after he died, I was poking around in his library room, in the empty room downstairs which is where he studied, where he kept some books and so forth."

"I was really looking for some connection at that time, to remember who he was I guess. I remember poking around, and looking through his old files and books and whatnot, and just trying to archeologize who he was. So I went up to the top shelf in the closet, and there I found the old Super 8 camera. I think I was age twelve at the time. And I decided to start fooling around with movies...start making some Super 8 films just because it was like this alchemic act, you know, this way to connect with him, really. To make movies, on his camera. That was the first inspiration. And it so happened, in the small town where I grew up in Ohio, there were a few of us young guys making Super 8 films in our back yards. There was kind of a little scene, actually, as it turned out."

So Rosette's very first attempts were carried out on this camera?

"Yeah. I started shooting Super 8 films on his camera, with friends in Ohio back yards. There were a few of us making movies, and I was also acting as best I could in other people's films–little impromptu back yard films, some of which were actually quite elaborate. It was always fun to take the cartridge of Super 8 film over to Barron's Drug Store...take it to the drug store and drop it off. And then a couple days later–four days later?–come back. Pay for it, take it home, go down to the basement, put it on the projector and see what you got."

"That part of movie making is great. But often missing now, with the instantaneous age, digital age, where we see all things immediately. It was great to have that forced anticipation, sort of waiting...enforced waiting period for the medium. Time was slower then, too, of course. As many others have pointed out, time is on an ever-increasing acceleration curve, which is linked to advances in technology and general world-speed."

And what of the importance of books?

"In terms of the books, where they came in...it was the physicality of the tome, of the book itself, that really had a kind of magic to it. A physical book is obviously much different texturally and physically than an eBook. As I said before, it was great to read books until I couldn't read anymore at night, until I was dead tired and just dropped off to sleep. And have this 'living object', this book, these books lying around like friendly cats, or family pets lying around. It felt comfortable...you know, it was great."

"Regarding Rimbaud and Céline, Journey to the End of the Night, A Season in Hell and Drunken Boat, I got into those guys, you know, in my college days, or thereabouts. Dylan Thomas is another story...actually my mother is from the UK, from Britain, originally–a scouser. Knew the Beatles when they were just starting off, when they were just one of many bands playing at the Cavern club. She's told us all many times how John Lennon would come around to everyone in the club, panhandling basically–but very cleverly. He'd ask everyone for 'tuppence' [two pence], saying something like, 'tuppence for a cup of coffee love?'. But by the time he'd have circulated through the whole club, he'd have enough for a full sandwich, the coffee of course, and all the fixings."

"Anyway, when we went over one time–I think I was about thirteen–the family took a trip over there and we went to Wales. We went to Dylan Thomas's boathouse, his writing house on the hill, on the cliff overlooking...I forget now if it was overlooking a valley or the sea. And the caretakers had left his space as it was, furnished as it was, like a time capsule. Kind of like this religious place...it felt like a well-lit, light place. Even though he drank his tits off, he had his passions and his torments, true. But, yeah, Dylan Thomas's boathouse left an impression on me."

It was an interesting coincidence. The filmmaker and I both had a British connection, and we'd both grown up only one town apart in northeast Ohio, as it would turn out. I felt that same, strange deja-vu feeling I'd had some months before, when I'd stumbled upon the old VHS tape of BookWars in the boxes of books. I ask Rosette to expand on his favorite books, wondering if we shared similar tastes.

"I went through a Kerouac phase, a Burroughs phase, as many of us do during our college years in the States. Céline's Journey to the End of the Night is really all I read by Céline, but I love the approach of that book, with the ellipses and the stream of consciousness. In fact, Rimbaud of course–I wish I could read French in order to really read him, but the translations I've read still convey that–how would you call it?–unplugged essence. Someone who is absolutely not even aware, I think, of even being a poet. He was what you would call the closest thing to a visionary shaman, in the area, environment, and time he was working."

"The Beats. Lawrence Ferlinghetti. Okay, quickly, yeah...when I was in San Francisco editing, doing the bulk of the editing on BookWars, of course I knew who Ferlinghetti was, and he was kind of a hero of mine, or at least I admired him. And I went to his bookstore many times in my post-college days, maybe eight or nine years before I'd been editing BookWars. So, when I found myself in his neighborhood again years later, making this movie, I thought: I've gotta' bring this movie over to him, I think he'd like it. I just had this feeling. Having been into the Beats, and the whole Beat sensibility myself."

I ask whether there were any face-to-face meetings.

"I met up with him a couple times; I mean, not planned meetings, and not one-on-one necessarily. He was always circulating through his store there in North Beach. And speaking of bootstrapping, Ferlinghetti certainly bootstrapped City Lights into existence, using a small internal publishing arm to support the emerging store, and vice versa. An interesting model. Anyway, one day I brought him a VHS tape. I didn't have time to label it properly, just scrawled the title on the label and brought it over to him..."

Immediately, I recalled the VHS tape of BookWars I'd found in an old box of books in my living room. The deja-vu feeling clutched at me again. Could it have been the same tape? The filmmaker's voice continued plainly from the machine:

"...then I remember going over there one day and asking–'Hey, what did you think of the movie?' And he said, 'Ah, man, yeah, it was kind of anarchistic.' And it was a gas to hear his reaction. Now, I didn't really think it was anarchistic myself, but I was still happy that he had a reaction to it. But, I would call BookWars more laissez faire; more like the loosely regulated Souk or market mentality which precedes a lot of the formalities of law and order that are imposed externally. In other words, you know, ancient market-style activity, which is not an anarchistic activity, but has its own, self-regulating order."

Does Rosette still love books?

"Love books? Yeah, I do love books. I do love books. I'm not a 'master literary scholar' of course, just because I made this or any other movie, or had written scripts and poems and whatnot. There's a lot I haven't read–it takes time to read, you know. And if you're working, and busting your ass to make a living, it's hard to find the time. Especially nowadays, where the treadmill seems to be running very, very fast. "'Time has teeth', as my friend Steve used to say. I've tried to listen to books on tape, you know, MP3s and audio books instead while I'm doing other mundane tasks. Sometimes that works; sometimes it doesn't. I think it's better to sit down actually, read a book and turn the pages. But you've got to find an environment with a forgiving financial overhead that offers you a bit of time."

7. THE ART BUFFET /"QUALITY OF LIFE" / THE GUY WITH THE CAMERA

Watching BookWars, I was struck by its revelatory effect, a display of many individual relationships with books and their varied meanings and importance. People feeding from the art buffet while struggling through existence. Even the somewhat annoying browsers who stand reading for extended periods tell us something. Most of all, I was genuinely disturbed to witness the effects of then-New York City Mayor Rudolph Giuliani's so-called "Quality of Life" campaign, which hit me as anti-art and fascist. A lust to kick out informal, unregistered entrepreneurs and other individuals–just have the cops pull them away. I'm curious whether any of the booksellers (off-stage, so to speak) pushed back, beyond cursing and having their books confiscated.

If so, was the filmmaker ever warned against filming by the police?

Rosette's response is both sobering and illuminating, and resonates with some of BookWars' darker moments. "I wouldn't say it was a lust to kick us out...or was it? It wasn't a lust. More like a–how would you call it?–a blanket mentality...what's the word for it? Where anyone who is–yes, as you say–'unregistered' must go, by definition. It was more robotic, regulation dispensed by an automaton. It was more like a lack of differentiation."

"It started, as everyone knows, legendarily at least, with the squeegee guys. The guys who would stand at stop lights and, when you stopped there, would run up and squeegee off your car windshield. Instead of just begging, they would squeegee it off. Cleaning it, in order to get some change...instead of just panhandling. Now, it's true, sometimes the squeegee juice was dirty, and they dirtied up the windshield more than it otherwise would have been. But, on the other hand, they were trying–some of them were actually trying. So it was a really gray area thing."

I mention that, to me, the Quality of Life campaign seemed ill-devised.

"There's a lot of literature and studies about the Quality of Life campaign, the nuts-and-bolts aspects, the below-the-line aspects of it. That was beyond the scope of this movie, insofar–especially as I wanted BookWars to be experiential, qualitative. About the look and feel of being out there, the feeling of that way of life, that slice in time. This is what we experienced as we experienced it. As mentioned in the movie, Sixth Avenue guys–they were hit harder by forces of the city, as implemented by the Sixth Precinct. Not only were they closer geographically to the Sixth Precinct building itself, but there must have been some degree of racial profiling going on, even if unconsciously."

"Also, their setups looked more improvised in some ways, you know...so it's about aesthetics, to the powers that be at least. Not that that bothered me. And not that that should matter. The guys on Sixth Avenue didn't have elaborate tables or setups. They weren't run-down either, just basic and to the point...and just by the nature of their business model they were often run-and-gun. They would set up quickly, put out the magazines, or books, and sell them. And they weren't provisioned, necessarily, by their business model to gussy up their tables to make them look like fancy book stalls, as some–not all–of us did on

West 4th, or on Third Avenue or uptown on the Upper West Side or wherever. Basically, you know, I would throw a nice-looking bed sheet, like with a pattern on it, like a maroon bed sheet. That was it. That was my thing that I had with polka dots on it–black polka dots...over the table, and it would drape over the front and give it the so-called extra veneer of aesthetic responsibility. And I don't know if it makes a difference or not."

This, however, was apparently not enough for the Quality of Life players.

"But anyway, it came quickly, and it was aligned–at least on West 4th Street–it was aligned with the university [NYU] working in the vicinity. They have significant real estate holdings, and they have some arguable interest in making the place look...campus-like. But the thing they forget is that it's not a campus, these are city streets. They run smack-dab into a conflict of interest right there. So you can imagine, if they own the outright campus, the hypothetical campus, then of course it makes sense that they have a right to ask people not to set up there. But you can't necessarily strong-arm people into not setting up on a public city street–it's not kosher. It's not bona fide behavior. But as we know in life, might often makes right, and they would call the police, you know, bring them out there to hassle us...and that went on for a while."

"There was a time...it actually became significant when they put planters down...some massive planters strategically placed just far apart enough so you couldn't set up a table. They also would spray paint these lines, arcane little lines that would change. Sometimes it was just a dot, or a little...and you couldn't quite figure out what it was. And that was on West 4th. On Third Avenue, where I sometimes set up, police came by without warning and they would kind of poke around. On Third Avenue, there was no methodology that I could discern."

How did the NYPD behave?

"Often, they were friendly, and went away after a while or after saying a few things about shortening or breaking down a table if you were stretched out too far. As you can see in the movie, they made Polish Joe nervous. Polish Joe tended to set up on Third Avenue by 11th Street. Over there, it was kind of a lone outpost area on the edge of the East Village where I also set up sometimes. The police presence there was random, but infrequent. On Sixth Avenue it was another story–like I said–and partly because, I think, of the business model of the booksellers over there. A bit more improvisational, a bit more run and gun. Some would say, well, why did they choose this business model? And the counterpoint to that would be, well, that was the business model available to them. That, if you have no other option, as many guys are starting up over there, you know, in a run-and-gun fashion, you don't necessarily have a sophisticated storage infrastructure, and vehicles and so forth, so it's going to look more run-and-gun. And that–when I say run-and-gun, I mean 'more improvised.'"

"But even so, they were often very clean set ups, you know, with the milk crates full of the books stacked at the end of the tables. There wasn't shit strewn across the sidewalk. Neat tables. I could see the guys took care of their items over there, so I think the reason for the heightened activity was because they were closer to the heart of the Sixth Precinct–Sixth Avenue. That was closer to the epicenter, the enforcement apparatus of the Mayor's Quality of Life program in that part of New York, and probably farther away from educated liberals that you might find on Astor Place or West 4th Street, or Third Avenue, who might object to booksellers being overtly hassled."

"There was most probably a racial profiling aspect to it as well, with the booksellers on Sixth Avenue being primarily people of color, African or Caribbean-American. But also, over there on Sixth Avenue, you had heavy pedestrian traffic, commercial traffic, and people passing by. Not really hanging out, but passing by, picking up a magazine and hurrying along. So there wasn't, as far as I could discern, a static liberal environment nearby to provide eyeballs to what was going on."

"Did any of the booksellers push back? Physically? No, how can you physically push back against the NYPD as a bookseller–throw a volume of Ayn Rand at them?"

"Generally the booksellers could not push back because, Number One, it was kind of pointless. You would go through the motions to try to get your book supply back. I had my books confiscated only one time. But, you have to blandly go through the motions to go get your stuff out of storage–police storage. You don't want to make waves where they could–in that environment, or situation, you're very vulnerable, you know. Your stock of books could mysteriously–quote unquote–'go missing.' And that's your livelihood. And then it goes missing on the way from the place where it was confiscated, to the holding area."

"But what you hear a lot of–and you hear this in

BookWars–you hear a lot of the friends of booksellers, the proxies, really bitching and shouting at the NYPD. There's a scene in BookWars on Sixth Avenue where one of the booksellers, who goes by the nickname 'Grady', he's getting his books confiscated, and you can hear a guy off screen shouting at the NYPD: 'You make your job hard. You make your own fucking job hard. 'Cause you're always doing foul shit to people. You make your own fucking job hard...' No violence though as far as I can discern. And, there was, well, on West 4th street an effort to organize. There were petitions made to the community board and so forth."

Was this period when the NYPD might have warned Rosette not to film any of the hassles?

"Was I warned by the police against filming? I wasn't warned in general terms; I was warned during specific incidents. Like that one incident on Sixth Avenue which I just mentioned, and which you can see in BookWars. You don't see the head of the shot, which is edited out because it just dragged on–I would have liked to include it, but it went on too long. It's in the B-roll archive. Anyway, on the tape you can see the officers looking directly at me, at the camera, and saying, 'Hey mister–mister–mister!' He was talking to me, he was looking at me. He obviously wanted me to stop shooting. And you could hear the guy, as mentioned earlier–the friend of Grady. Grady is the nickname of the guy who was busted, as I mentioned, and who wheeled his books away in BookWars."

"Anyway, you can hear Grady's colleague, his friend, who had been already giving some shit to the officers. You can hear him say, 'Hey, he can film if he wants, it's a free society!' Something like that. I have to look at the B-roll again."

"So I just kept shooting when they were taking the books–whenever I saw that. There were a couple episodes...a couple incidents where I went by during the peak of my shooting. I guess by then I was known as 'The Guy With The Camera', and they, the NYPD also knew I was a bookseller too, which made things interesting. As if I were I was a renegade street bookseller-filmmaker with a camera! That's the thing, but in a different neighborhood."

"Even so, I could see on a couple occasions the cops gathered–assembling–as if to do something over there, and then I showed up with the camera...not even rolling, just hanging. It was hanging. I had like a sling for it, around my shoulder. And they could see me and the camera, and they would kind of disassemble and murmur, hang out for a while and then just dissipate. I wouldn't even be shooting, just lingering around with my camera. That happened a couple times. And that was before smartphones were ubiquitous...before smartphones with cameras were invented! Which is the sort of thing that would happen now. But back then there were no smartphones. So, when 'The Guy With the Camera' showed up, it did change the dynamic."

8. THE QUEST: OHIO TO NEW MEXICO TO L.A. TO SAN FRANCISCO

The bootstrapping filmmaker endured and worked freelance gigs and odd jobs in an extended and ongoing post-production effort in New Mexico, Los Angeles, San Francisco–then headed to New York again to revisit fellow booksellers and shoot some more, before heading back to San Francisco to edit again. As if that weren't enough, he headed back to New York in order to complete the final edit. This 'ping-ponging' around the country must have been as grueling as the original shoot.

I ask if the idea of framing the documentary within a "man heading out West to start anew" concept occurred during these very long back-and-forth road trips, or was it there from the start?

"Let me address the [framing] device first, the road trip. Because the story is driven by a narrator relating his experiences, I thought it would be appropriate to have some situation where a narrator would be talking to a friend, or colleague, or fellow traveler and sort of support that storytelling device. And so then I thought, well, in what situation does a person elaborate on a long chapter of their life...where they've just been, or where they're going? At that time, I was doing a lot of ride shares. Not just road trips for fun and being a bohemian, but actually relocating for work, or to gather books from distant sources, or to locate the editing systems I needed. That's how I got around, for the majority of it. You connect with someone on Craigslist or some other rideshare resource who happens to need a ride where you're going, or who's going your way, and you hit the road together."

"Why? Well, because it was cheaper that way. Remember, that's how it goes when you're bootstrapping it. And, you know, when you do a ride share, you share the driving and the cost of gas, usually with a stranger who happens to be going your way. So, naturally, you get to talking to while away the hours-and the stranger transitions into a colleague or a friend-a 'Camerado'-by the end of the journey. So that became the nominal, assumed format for the narrated intro and outro of BookWars. It was kind of an instinctive choice, based on those experiences."

"Anyway, there was a hell of a lot of driving. For example, from New York to Albuquerque, when I set out to make the first assembly edit, back in '96 or so. As winter was approaching, I packed up my stuff, all the tapes and material I had shot so far, and hit the road in my Japanese jalopy. I think it was an old Datsun. I stopped off in Ohio where I grew up, and worked for a stint-this is while I'm gearing up to go to New Mexico. I needed to find work to fund my trip and to finance the next stage of the edit, but at the time-winter in Ohio-job opportunities were not exactly falling off the trees. But there was one job that materialized, maybe because no one else wanted it or they felt it was too strange."

"There was this guy who was in jail. He was in-I've never experienced this before-this guy who was in jail, but they let him out on work release each day. A carpenter; and he was a decent guy. He was in jail for DWI. I needed work, and this job came up. I think no one else wanted the job because the guy was-quote unquote-in jail. He was a very soft-spoken nice guy. He wasn't like, you know, a 'criminal'-whatever that means. But that was my only job lead at the time, and it was starting to snow at that point, and I needed to gather money to get out to New Mexico to make the first edit."

"While it was snowing I'd go out, pick him up from the county jail before dawn, when it was still dark and the roads were slick and thick with snow. And my flimsy car had no decent defrost, so at times, many times, I either had to drive with my head out the window so I could see better, or had to just 'wing it' based on the relative glow of the lights in my windshield indicating where the oncoming cars were."

"Only once, once I recall, did I have absolutely no idea where I was on the road. It was snowing hard, a big Ohio snowstorm, a huge truck was coming my way, and it was pitch black, but the headlights of the truck were blinding, just hitting my frosted, iced-up windshield and illuminating the whole thing with a blinding, spectral glow. I couldn't see anything. I had no idea where the road or the oncoming truck was. I just had to hope for the best. The truck passed very close to my car, I could feel the impact of the air blast coming from it, pushing me off to the other side of the road. That was a tough and strange moment–very memorable though."

"Anyway, I made it to the county jail each morning to pick up the carpenter. Then, as soon he got out of the jail- I don't know how he got it, or had it, but he would take a deep and powerful bong hit! That's right...he kept it in the glove compartment of his car which was parked not far from the jail. That was his morning 'Bong Hit of Freedom.' And then we'd head down to Cleveland, to where he had these mysterious carpentry jobs lined up."

"We'd go to these incredibly rough, weird neighborhoods I'd never been to when growing up, neighborhoods we'd just passed by on the highway on the way to 'Grandma's House'. And I'd help this guy do these strange carpentry jobs. One house we were working at was located just across an empty lot from a steel factory. The empty lot next to us was full of Amish workers, scurrying to rebuild this other house which had blown up after a massive gas explosion. The Amish guys had already built the entire house once, and nearly completed it, when apparently a massive gas explosion had flattened it completely. They were starting again from scratch. It was like the story of Sisyphus."

"Anyway, I was basically the guy who picked up this carpenter from jail. And I assisted with the carpentry too, so I guess I was technically hand to have there on the site working as well. And I gained an extra skill set too. But he was thinking of it from his point of view: he was happy to get out from jail each day and go to work, and it didn't matter, I could've been a fucking chimpanzee as long as I could pick him up and drove the car! But it so happened that, you know, I was the guy available...and so we worked together. And I needed the money to fund my trip so I could get to New Mexico and make the assembly edit of the movie. That's another story in itself."

I say it all sounds fairly exhausting, having to balance these very different tasks and experiences.

"Yeah, overall, it was grueling. But that's bootstrapping it. There was no alternative. There was a lot of travel. Looking back, it was completely not rational. The whole process. It wasn't like...a normal, mechanized, commercial-industrial process. But it was the only way to get the movie done. And, of course I was driven to make the movie for artistic fulfillment, whatnot. But it would also be vital for building my portfolio and having a shot at making other funded movies later–without guarantees of course! Like many things in life, it's a guessing game to some degree and you have to feel it out, the process and relative payoffs, etcetera."

"But, once I had made the decision to execute the project, the movie, I was driven by almost like a madness. It was more than a passion. I felt driven to get it to each subsequent step. I felt, for example, driven to get to New Mexico to make the assembly edit. Had to get there–any way I could. And so, each step had its own driving force, and I was only thinking about the next step, and nothing else. I guess that's what enabled me to get through the project, through the bootstrapping of that movie."

"Because if I had taken it all en masse...if I–as I do now, sometimes, when I look back now in reflection and I say to myself, 'How the fuck did I do that?'... if I had looked at the entire process, laid out end to end over the years and the incredible demands and struggle and sacrifice it would require...I would never have been able to do it. So, if you're bootstrapping a project and it's getting really tough: just don't look at the whole thing. Just slog through each step. Put blinders on, turn off your long-term thinking, and execute, like a maniacal robot."

"That movie, BookWars, should not have been made at all. I mean, there was no funding. There was no equipment. I had no camera. I was not from a connected background. It was virtually impossible; the editing equipment was expensive and hard to access at the time."

"Regarding the step-by-step approach: as each step was concluded, it also became more and more tantalizing, and achievable, to go to the next step. For example, I did the assembly edit of BookWars in Albuquerque, on Super Bowl Sunday...I think that was 1996. With the crowd there, the way they reacted to it, and the way the material played, I realized, 'Well, this is an interesting milieu...this is an interesting scene on the streets of New York that will never otherwise be seen or brought to light in the same way.' I didn't quite realize it when I was back in New York, because I was in it. I was working there within it and couldn't see this significance of that slice of life objectively. Yet, once I was in New Mexico, I was able to stand back from the material a bit and appraise it objectively. And I had to continue."

Did being much younger have a hand in more readily accepting–or ignoring–considerable risks?

"At the time–what was I, 28? I was in my mid-twenties when I was shooting it, and starting to edit it. So you know how it is. In your mid-twenties, anything goes. You can still afford to be a bit of a bohemian or gypsy, and live on couches and so forth. Unfortunately, I was still living on couches much later as a result of the expenses involved in making the movie, and that was not fun at all. I'll get to that later. But, at the time I was in my 20s; it was my first feature documentary. I had done Charlie's Box, a 16mm psychological noir drama beforehand, and of course numerous movies at NYU Film School and before that when I was growing up in Ohio. But BookWars was a suitable, bigger project to bite into, which could viably lead to the next step in my moviemaking career. Since I was younger and in my 20's, I floated and rolled with the project without making any thorough market survey or assessment of my cash flow, finances, or livelihood. Luckily I made it through, but looking back I wouldn't advise that approach. It's too careless and can lead to crippling debt. But it's easy to do that in your 20s. And the movie was ultimately finished when I was 30."

"Quickly going back to the device of the road trip...that did come from my frequent road trips, either solo, or with other ride share people. But the 'Man heading out West', that's an iconic American thing–North American thing at least–the idea of heading out West to start anew. And I had actually bought into that many times during my youth, going out West to have some kind of adventure. And it is, actually, or it was at least at the time, at the time looser and freer out West. Especially in the Southwestern USA, in those big expanses, those giant beautiful valleys and so forth, you know. When you cross the Mississippi for the first time, it's a fabulous feeling. And it does feel freer out there. I can make a somewhat reasoned comparison because I lived in New York about ten years in total, which makes me a 'real New Yorker'-at least according to [former New York Mayor] Ed Koch! I mean, I went to school there, and slugged it out in New York doing movie projects, selling books of course, and so forth. I was there about ten years total. Anyway in my view the West has a more open, airy feeling of freedom to it."

My own Western-and Eastern-travels align with Rosette's perceptions; I ask if life in Asia is as interesting as I imagine.

"Well, of course it's a world apart, very different, more than I can sum up here in this bootstrapping story, I reckon. Funny though, talking about that device of 'heading out West to start anew'. In Southeast Asia, Buddhist countries, such as Cambodia, Thailand, maybe Laos too...the West in Asian mythology is viewed as a place of death. It's not a place of renewal, but the mythical place or direction of death."

"But, story-wise in my movie, the 'Man Heading Out West' adheres to the North American frontier mythology of renewal. I didn't just do it as a goofy gimmick. I did it because I actually had headed out West previously and experienced that flush feeling of freedom. So I injected that into the film as part of the device. I needed–and wanted–a storytelling device to justify the narration. Because I'm not really necessarily into first-person documentaries as much as some others are. There's a whole school of first-person documentaries where the filmmaker makes movies, constantly, about themselves and their own life, and talk about themselves a lot. And it can be interesting, I think, if you're fascinating to begin with, but a lot of the stuff I've seen...they're not always that fascinating to be honest."

"And so, I didn't necessarily want to make a first-person documentary that featured myself incessantly. There is a school, a style of personal documentary which frequently utilizes this approach, but that's not really my cup of tea. With BookWars, I wanted people to think Oh, it's the guy. It's the narrator. Not, it's the filmmaker, Jason Rosette. In fact, aside from my appearance as one of the street booksellers, I would have preferred to be completely invisible. In order to do that, I needed to create a device, and wanted to create a device, and so I chose the device of the narrator telling a story as a recollection on an extended road trip with a stranger (as with a ride share).

"I guess it could have been something else, like a guy ascending in a hot air balloon or an airplane with someone else, and undertaking a journey that way. Hot air balloon? Well you get what I mean. But our device happened to be the road trip, because that was more appropriate, based on the modes of travel I had been experiencing in my own life."

"And let's not forget, that's how a lot of the book-gathering was done in the later stages. Initially, it was done by going to thrift stores and, you know, little used book shops and whatnot. Later on when I got my first car in New York, my first jalopy, it expanded my range and a lot of time was spent on the road going to get books. So, getting the books...going, say, from New York–Manhattan–to Ithaca, in upstate New York. That was like a big once-a-year sale, up in Ithaca, and it was like a legendary, massive book sale. You needed to drive from New York to Ithaca, which is not that far, really. It's still New York State, but it's a road trip. You need to stay overnight and buy a carload of books to make the trip worthwhile."

"I remember I stayed up there, and I slept in my car in

a polar sleeping bag because I had the old Japanese station wagon and I didn't want to spend money on a motel. It was really cold, though. I remember now. I went from Ithaca...went from New York to Ithica, then one year, I continued straight up to Toronto, by way of Niagara Falls, because we have some family up there. And I'm parked next to Niagara Falls with this jalopy-my beat up Japanese station wagon-packed to the gills and sagging, absolutely stuffed, with really a nice haul of beautiful books. I remember standing there at the rail looking out over the Horseshoe Falls with the mist and vapor wrapping around me and the car and the books. That was a very memorable slice of time, a moment."

"Yeah, so there's a lot of road trips involved in bookselling too. At least according to the business model that I employed, and that the folks I knew on Third Avenue, even Upper West Side, and West 4th Street did. The guys on Sixth Avenue were more into scavenging, or flipping books and material much more quickly. Different business model. They didn't need a car. They were bootstrapping their businesses using completely different methods."

9. NAKED LUNCH / A SNAKE IN THE GARDEN

Having once experienced the painful necessity to sell part of my personal library, I completely "get"-and inhabit-the reality of book addiction, and found it interesting that William Burroughs' Naked Lunch is mentioned in BookWars. That book about addiction (to many things, including power and violence) being itself a favorite among certain book addicts has a pleasing resonance with Jason Rosette's film. Akin to plans against the street booksellers, authorities tried to ban Naked Lunch and failed. My somewhat conspiratorial theory is that BookWars, lacking "official" sanction, might very well have been targeted for daring to show street-level love of, and fascination with, unbridled art and information-the same goal with trying to shut down the vendors. I ask Rosette to share his thoughts on these ruminations.

"I don't know if I'm supposed to comment on Naked Lunch in this question, and/or the potential conspiracy. But let me just sweep through the questions. Naked Lunch is a favorite–was a favorite–in that part of town, over on West 4th Street and the 'middle part' of the Village. Also on Astor Place and Third Avenue. Those were the areas that I sold, but mostly on West 4th. And in the Village–you know, Greenwich Village–there's a huge and rich countercultural tradition. You could obviously refer to Naked Lunch as a countercultural work, whether it's about addiction or not. I see it, as well as the rest of Burroughs' books as...first and foremost, as a countercultural work. And then the addiction aspects become apparent as you start reading it. The New Yorker, by the way, when they reviewed BookWars, mentioned the addictive properties of books in their review, now that we're talking about Naked Lunch and addiction."

"And so, yes, the whole notion of being addicted to books is like an armature that the movie swings around, sure. And that's very...it's honorable to be able to dispense Naked Lunch as part of my trade at the time. Yes. Texas Tom, I believe it was, he also mentions specifically in that shot where you see the World Trade Center in the background, shot back before 9/11 of course...Tom was one of our frequent customers. He's the one in the movie who said, 'Yeah, books are more like an addiction.'"

"It's true; and even actually the physicality of the books is an addiction. Collecting books...the stories I could tell you about people who bought books. They passed by the bookstand, and just got tangled in the web of book addiction and bought six or seven books at a time. It's inconceivable that they would have the time to read them. So there's something more to it, to the properties of books, than just accumulating knowledge. There is the aspect of the qualitative physical presence in the digital age."

"That, by the way, seems to be the future direction of the eBook, or its electronic or bio-mechanical successor–in the future, the successor of the eBook will just be some kind of vehicle, physical or digital or a hybrid of the two, that injects pure knowledge into one's head. Even today, you have the two different extremes. You have the book itself–a physical, qualitative property with a weight, a smell, and some texture–and you have pure knowledge in the electronic format, which will perhaps in the distant future be just injected electronically into your head. Those are the two antipodes really."

We'd sidetracked a bit, so I sought to get back to the interaction between the authorities and the sidewalk booksellers. I also ask if my conspiracy theory about BookWars being singled out by authorities holds any water.

"Regarding this whole thing about BookWars being targeted, the production being targeted, well, it's possible. However, looking objectively at the situation, New York is a massive city, and one independently produced documentary...I don't think that would have tripped any wires in [then-Mayor] Giuliani's office, to be honest. I mean, it would be tempting to think ego-wise, if one must grasp at that, that it would cause a stink or a dustup of some kind. I don't think it did. I think they had so many other things on their plate, you know. It would be different if someone big, like Steven Spielberg or Christopher Nolan or J.J. Abrams, were making such a movie in a scaled-up Hollywood setting. 'Hey, Steven Spielberg is making a movie about how sidewalk booksellers in New York are getting hassled!' That level of Hollywood production would have tripped wires in the mayor's office. I don't think BookWars tripped wires, at least in the administrative level. Maybe on the local level, among police officers. But again, the eyeballs on the street, on West 4th, Third Avenue, and Astor Place were largely significant enough to sort of dissuade the police."

"I mean, there's also...you could call it a profiling issue. I'm a white guy, though I am not from a rich family, basically working class background. Going back really far, I guess I have some North African, some Spanish, some Black Irish, Polish, whatever. Anyway, there were some black guys that worked on West 4th Street, by the way, and some Hispanic and Latino guys as well. So it wasn't just white bread over there on West 4th, or Third Avenue. The cops could have come for us more frequently; they did come, actually, and I got broken down, forced to break down my tables a number of times and had to stash my books. But I think we were hassled less in that part of town as well because of the eyeballs–eyeballs of customers, eyeballs on the street. Remember, this is before the day of the smartphone, where everything can go viral, video-wise."

"So you have the eyeballs–physical, actual living eyeballs on the street in the form of customers at the tables, who are willing to articulate and perhaps intervene in the event that the local-level authorities were out of line."

"I don't sense that that was the case on Sixth Avenue, at least to that degree. Sixth Avenue was much a much more urbanized part of town. It was not necessarily a 'designated bohemian area', as one may consider the Washington Square park area, or Astor place or 3rd avenue. It was an urban commercial fast zone, and a lot of people sweeping through. Hence the business model was different over there, and the products they were selling. You know, fashion magazines and so forth."

"The sellers there were more attuned toward that commercial zone with the bulk of people zipping through in a hurry on their way to get somewhere. So, it's possible that concerned customers were just not as static, just not hanging out en masse as they were on West 4th street or Third Avenue or the Upper West Side, for instance. And as a result, if that were the case, they would thereby provide fewer eyes on the street to take note of the situation and intervene or comment if and when the authorities arrived to hassle someone."

"I don't think BookWars was targeted in some way by Giuliani or the administration. No, I don't. What I do know, verifiably, is that BookWars sustained its most significant interference–ironically, perhaps–from a separate, unaffiliated sociology book project about sidewalk booksellers, another street bookseller project that was happening simultaneously while I was doing the final pick-up shooting for our movie. That other project was focusing mainly on the Sixth Avenue booksellers, so our overlap was modest. Theirs was not a documentary; it was a sociology textbook called Sidewalk, being written with the backing of a well-established, pretty massive publisher–Farrar, Straus and Giroux. Well, they did have a video component in the works, but the book itself seemed to be the core of their project. Those guys, that team, did not embrace the fact that BookWars had been in the works and was shooting around their–quote unquote–territory."

"One of their key stakeholders and participants was very hostile, really to an irrational degree, and that person unfortunately undertook some damaging outreach to participants in the BookWars effort and members of the press. But I can get in to that a bit more later."

"But the NYPD did not interfere with BookWars as a result of any prompting from the unaffiliated project. The movement by the authorities was a cultural attack. Part of a meta-cultural shift in the attitude of the city, possibly the entire USA, I think, a tilt against the "unregulated'. It was more like...interference on the cultural level. As mentioned, there was some behind-the-scenes, below-the-line level interference, which came from Sidewalk, the sociology textbook project. They didn't want us around; they didn't want BookWars around. In the end, strings were pulled by that project to interfere with BookWars, leading up to and after its release, primarily through ties with The New York Times and some of the other cultural echelons of the city."

"This is doubly unfortunate, because BookWars is and was a real bona-fide project in favor of New York City, in favor of the quality of life of the public forum. BookWars was supporting the cultural aspects of New York which, now we can see fifteen years later, are becoming diminished. People are lamenting the disappearance of street life in American cities, the increasingly corporate look and feel of New York, the departure of artists and so forth. The movie should have been celebrated by The New York Times, not attacked. Luckily, the New York Film Critics Circle, the New Yorker, Time Out New York, and many others all had very positive things to say about the movie. But that's part of bootstrapping a project like we did–it's not going to be a smooth ride, you can bet on that."

10. ADDICTION / SOCIOLOGICAL WARFARE IN THE PUBLIC FORUM

The campaign was disruptive, but didn't succeed in completely dismantling the street booksellers. Does Jason Rosette recall if those involved in the textbook publisher-backed project were similarly harassed? They probably were, but I'm curious.

"Yes, the booksellers themselves on Sixth Avenue, as can be seen in the movie BookWars, were harassed...they received the brunt of the activity. I don't know if the word harassed is appropriate but, yes, they received the brunt of the crackdown and their books were taken more frequently, and they were told to break down more frequently–for a variety of reasons. Probably because, as I mentioned before, there were fewer static, ambient book lovers that were hanging around. By nature of Sixth Avenue, it was much more of a kinetic environment where people were passing by quickly to get–maybe not even thinking of getting a book or a magazine–but they saw the sellers' tables and then stopped to get them. It was foot traffic, you know, that drove Sixth Avenue. So, the community of people that bought books were far less likely to be hanging around to keep track of, or to monitor, the police."

"And so, you know, you can also look at the racial dimension of it and say, well, was it racial profiling? Probably, and mainly. There were Latino and Black booksellers on West 4th and over also on Third Avenue, Astor Place, and as far as I know, even St. Mark's–it got to be even more minority oriented with those ad hoc setups on St. Mark's Place."

"But in terms of aesthetics, the Sixth Avenue booksellers generally had well-organized setups. They were selling with clean tables, overall, with their stock of books stacked neatly beneath. Bootstrapping their businesses in decent fashion. Yet they received the brunt of that crackdown in that vicinity. And the activity of the book project being written about them seemed to have little bearing, either way. The researcher of that book, the professor Mitch Duneier who was doing participant observation on Sixth Avenue was, to my perception and observation...he was not around at night time. He would usually go home, or wherever he went, at dusk. And the booksellers themselves stayed out. So I don't know what bearing, if any at all, that particular book project had on the exposure of the 6th avenue booksellers vis-a-vis the authorities in that area."

So none of the team from the book project were harassed?

"I don't recall any participants from the publisher-backed project being harassed. But I did–with my own eyes, and camera–observe two, that is Slim, who's real name is Mudrick, and his colleague Grady, being broken down. The NYPD telling them to break down their tables. And in Grady's case, as can be seen in the movie BookWars, his stuff was confiscated. So, people can elaborate and extrapolate as to why they received more of a crackdown than folks in other parts of the Village or on the Upper West Side, or whatnot. And it was probably–in my view–it was probably due to two main reasons. Number One: those guys were closer to Sixth Precinct, and Sixth Precinct NYPD was circulating a lot more frequently up Sixth Avenue. And secondly, there is a people-of-color racial profiling component too, which could be added to the formula."

"There also were more people of color on Sixth Avenue, or primarily, versus West 4th or Third Avenue, Astor Place, and Upper West Side. So it could arguably be a profiling issue as well. So, the short answer is, 'yes, the guys on Sixth Avenue–as I said in the movie–got hit the hardest': repeatedly, far more frequently. I don't know, actually, if Mitch–the professor writing the textbook–if that researcher had been out during those times when the police came and confiscated the books of the Sixth Avenue booksellers...would the NYPD have restrained themselves? I don't know. In fact, I noticed that researcher leaving usually at around dusk, not generally staying out later than dusk."

"You know, night time is a different story. I mean, the folks on Sixth Avenue often stayed out all night. I stayed out on W4th street all night a few times, just to make sure I had a spot on a big day. Whether they were actively selling or not is another story. But on West 4th Street, usually folks would pack up at the end of the day. Occasionally, hardcore booksellers would stay out with their tables wrapped in plastic, indicating down-time, and the seller might be sitting in their car or sleeping in a van, or something. Or having a street helper monitor the table while they were gone. But usually things were broken down at night on West 4th, where they were not on Sixth Avenue. It was more of like a perpetual stretch of selling, punctuated by times being absent and presumably collecting more material, more content to sell."

Hearing all of this, I admit my conspiracy theory is invalid. But I think the culturally based attack is even worse, and ever sadder.

"The unexpected, and uninvited, interference," says Rosette," coming from the Farrar, Strauss, Giroux funded sociology book project was really unfortunate stuff which actually worked against the cultural tapestry and life of New York City. Permanently, I think."

"I don't think that the mayor's office targeted BookWars. No, for us it was probably haphazard local-level NYPD guys. I don't think the university–NYU–was that happy about BookWars being made and possibly revealing any of the nuts-and-bolts, inner workings of what was going on in their neighborhood, vis-a-vis the hassling of the street booksellers in the area."

"Even so, I wasn't there to slam NYU or to do investigative reporting. As I said before, I went to school there and I found some value in several aspects of the film program where I studied. Which is why I chose not to mention the university by name in the movie–the name wasn't important, just the general proposition that a university, any university, could be have in that way. It was more like the dynamic; the 'player of the university,' that was important, that general actor and stakeholder. Hence I didn't need to name them. Just that they were a player in that part of town, a very wealthy player with a lot of real estate holdings, and some interest in sculpting or provisioning the way their environment looked, for a myriad of reasons. And so, that was their interest."

Did NYU summon the cops?

"The university would verifiably call the cops to hassle us at times. How do I know this? From first-person experience. A couple times the cops showed up and said: 'Well, we're gettin' calls from the university.' So, the university had a direct line to the Sixth Precinct, and would hassle booksellers on its doorstep to try to push them out of the way."

"I don't think the university was ideologically opposed

to booksellers on the street. I think what it was, ultimately, was a cosmetic thing. They wanted their immediate front doorstep to Washington Square Park to be more campus-like, and squeaky clean. On one hand that's understandable; on the other hand: it's not a private campus. That's a public city street...so you need to go through the proper channels. And they also should respect the public forum."

"The public forum is not a quaint hippy joke, by the way. Without the public forum, without an active, viable public forum, your city will die. Your environment will die."

"Without a public forum; without a living public forum, the city will die. It's like a coral reef. I recall diving in Dahab in Egypt , near the Blue Hole, and later in Honduras and in Mexico–a few very deep dives and wreck dives too.

And every time, whenever I encountered a reef, a large developed coral reef, I always thought it resembled a kind of city. Maybe that was New York City, lingering there in side me even fifty meters beneath the sea. But unfortunately, I think–although I haven't lived in New York full-time for a while–in part because of my experiences after having made BookWars which I'll get to in a minute–the cultural street-life...the cultural life of the city has been diminished to some degree from what my friends back there tell me here and there. I mean, there are plenty of articles discussing how 'Artists are leaving New York' and so forth."

"Well, you know, it starts with the street. It starts with the public forum. When the public becomes cleansed beyond a reasonable point, becomes sanitized, then part of the life of the city dies. I mean, I'm not...I don't want to get into the "squeegee guy" argument. But, street booksellers, whether on West 4th or Sixth Avenue, are part of the cultural life of the city–period. I can say that with confidence. And when they are pushed away, there is a negative effect–I mean, look at them, they're selling books!"

"Obviously, people can disagree or agree. By the way, if anyone does disagree with any of these items, there's no need to gossip or moan. Send me an email, whether you support my position or not. You know, let's be transparent and open and direct about it. I'll try to set up some kind of forum on the website or whatnot, or you can write about it in the review section of the eBook, or the audio book, whatever may become of this.

11. OFF-SEASON / SELF-SUFFICIENCY / 9-11 RECOLLECTIONS

The "off-season" material in BookWars is interesting and entertaining: Rick getting magic trick gigs, Pete gingerly shampooing and grooming cats, and the filmmaker working in New Mexico on a Western, The Desperate Trail. He spent a lot of time with these individuals, and must have had some great conversations. I ask Rosette if he came away with any enduring insights and/or wisdom:

"I think the wisdom, or insights, comes from the nature of the job. As a street bookseller, I was working with a really eclectic group of people, folks who are also out on the street selling books in a massive public forum-

New York City, Manhattan. And there's a tremendous, vibrant stream of people passing by the bookstand. And I gained insight and wisdom and perspective from having conversations with a lot those people whether they were regulars or just people stopping by to browse as a one-off."

"So, answering the question: the biggest gem of wisdom has something to do with being self-sufficient. Self-sufficiency. That would be it. I learned to be really self-sufficient, amongst a-quote unquote-tribe of others who were similar to me. With different backgrounds, of course, as you can see in the movie. Different motivations. Different aims in life. But there was that commonality. So, of all the people I knew and met-let me divide them, I guess, into two parts. The booksellers-the fellow booksellers-and the non-booksellers of the public form. Customers, riffraff of the street, police authorities, whatnot."

"Let me start with the booksellers. Most of the booksellers-all, actually-that I knew were drawn to that occupation unconsciously or consciously out of a need or desire to be self-sufficient. To have some control over their destiny. It's still going on, there's still bookselling being done in New York, from what I hear. I recently contacted Pete–Pete Whitney, the King of the Booksellers on West 4th street–we're in touch. And he says, 'Yeah, some guys are still out there. Zack is still out there,' and so forth, a few others."

"So there're still some booksellers out there. Pete actually is not doing much bookselling; these days he's working in the scenic department of various movies, and TV, in New York. He's still maintaining his massive stash of books in his warehouse in Newark, I suppose, as a hedge against variables in the economy. Pete is really a master of being self-sufficient, and I would see him as a symbol of self-sufficiency. At least from my close contact working over on West 4th Street. But Joe–Polish Joe–who sold on Third Avenue, was also very self-sufficient in a different way. And I could observe the same qualities over on Sixth Avenue with the booksellers over there."

"It seemed like everyone who was selling books was doing it as a means of being self-sufficient. In an economy which, and a culture which doesn't offer a lot of opportunities for that. I can compare it, by way of example, to Asia, where I've spent a lot of time and where I am now. In Asia it's exceedingly common for people to set up a little food stand, or a shoeshine stand, or a key making stand, without any regulation at all. It's laissez faire economy."

"In the States, especially, there seems to be less cultural space for laissez faire economy in terms of a micro-business with minimal regulation and startup costs. Which is what we were doing as sidewalk booksellers. It didn't seem like there were many–looking back–it didn't seem like there were many options in that environment and in the States in general, to be in control of one's economic destiny in that way. But that was paradoxically one of the ostensible, original driving aims of the American way. I mean, the bootstrapping pioneers in America were all...that was their driving impulse. Their impetus was to be self-sufficient, to stake a claim. And to make a name for oneself; to be something, to make a living for oneself without being hassled by the authorities or the powers-that-be."

I comment that in BookWars there are many moments when the viewer can see the intensity of engagement in the vendors' expressions–genuine heart-to-heart and mind-to-mind exchanges with customers and browsers alike.

"I could see that instinct, that drive, there in the sidewalk booksellers. So the insight I have gained from that occupation and experience hinges around the notion of self-sufficiency in America, which is a hugely textured subject, multilayered of course. It seems...comparing Asia to the United States for instance–reflecting back on that time–that there's a tremendous amount of regulation in the States, from local government levels, on the state level, on the federal level. And this is not necessarily the case in other parts of the world. And I think the impulse, or need, or desire to be self-sufficient is part...part of human nature, it's ingrained into human nature. That is to have the desire and actionable option to go out and make a living for oneself–to be self-sufficient. To determine one's own economic fate; to know and understand–and this is important–to know and understand the rules that are governing one's economic fate. That's really important."

"Because, from what I can gather now, that does not seem to be the direction that America is going these days. I've been back to the States, of course, many times while working in Asia–I was working with the State Department and U.S. Embassy in Yangon [Rangoon, Burma] as I mentioned, so I continue to be an active American, even while I'm abroad. And recently went back to interview for a federal government position. And, while I was there, I was also looking and probing for other jobs and so forth. It seemed to me that the only alternative, though, if you are not able to find a standard regulated job in America, in order to be self-sufficient and in control of one's economic destiny with minimal startup capital, is to do something online–which is great. But then of course, in that instance, the idea of the physical, geographical bordered 'state' is diminished."

"To be able to set up a business with a minimum of regulation and startup capital, which is what we had as sidewalk booksellers, and still make a contribution to society. And to do that with a minimum of regulation–is a fabulous thing. I think that's part of the initial 'intoxication feeling' that is evident in the movie. That a person could go out there into the public forum, and set up their own micro-business, really, with a minimum of regulation. It's bootsrapping, and it's Freedom. Make some cash; pay their rent; pay their bills, make an honest living, doing something fairly interesting, with some mental and entrepreneurial involvement, and still be valued in the community. I'm talking about legit sidewalk booksellers, not those few who fence stolen art books or other books. which regrettably happened here and there."

"I think that market mentality, the ancient souk

mentality, is missing from the American experience to a significant degree. These days–it seems to be more and more evident each time I go back to the U.S.–I could not discern many places that were 'unregulated'. Yeah, you could go to a flea market and rent a stand and, you know, get a space. But that's largely regulated."

I wondered: when Beat-generation legend Lawrence Ferlinghetti commented that he found BookWars "Anarchistic"...could he have been referring to this form of laissez faire self-sufficiency?

"I think what Lawrence Ferlinghetti was talking about when he said the movie was 'anarchistic'...I don't think he meant that in a Guy Fawkes sort of anarchism–a chaotic or destructive anarchism, or whatever you want to call it. He was talking more about living life by your own rules as much as possible. As closely as possible as can be achieved in a modern mechanized, industrialized developed nation. That is, going and setting up a table with books, worthy physical items you've acquired and curated–used books. And setting up shop without being regulated, but still doing so in a respectful, self-moderating and polite way. The utter simplicity and freedom of it is brilliant."

"I had done other jobs before and since then. Including of course working on productions, shooting and editing videos, working as a screenwriter and script doctor, the list goes on. The sidewalk bookselling, that was the one occupation I've had where regulation was really almost completely absent. But it was self-regulating. That's what's interesting."

"The booksellers would, you know, keep an eye on each other's tables. Nobody would make a big mess, you know. Other booksellers would intervene and kind of prod and poke that person to behave. I've seen that in different parts of town. Wherever it would be: on Sixth Avenue, generally, the setups are quite tidy. On West 4th Street as well. And even on Third Avenue and Astor Place. Now during the late 80s and early 90s, if you went as far as, like, St. Mark's Place in the East Village, you started to find really scattered setups along St. Mark's. Where people were just selling junk, selling books laid out on the sidewalk without any propriety or consideration for the environment. That is where I see it sort of ebbed off, and started to enter the world of being somewhat wanton. But that was only on the frontier, over by St. Mark's and beyond."

Did any people simply walking by ever complain

about the booksellers' presence?

"The nominal, established clusters of sidewalk booksellers always seemed to be self-regulating and maintaining their own code, their own way, which did not realistically impede the life of any passerby or even a nearby business. Not as far as I could discern. I mean, I can't recall any instance where a bookstore nearby complained about us. And conversely, we would know better than to set up–you would not set up a table of used books right outside a used book store. It just wasn't proper. And this inner knowledge, or code, I've seen it in other environments as well, where regulation, external governance, was lacking."

"I think quickly back to 9/11. I was in New York on 9/11. I was living up on Morton street at the time and as soon as I knew out what happened, I went down and volunteered right away. I was carrying buckets of Gatorade and water, and little trays of snacks and stuff down into the pit, into Ground Zero where the firemen were clawing away. Sometimes literally with their hands. And they needed Gatorade; they were always asking for Gatorade...they were asking for water, for sweets, for chocolate. It was the adrenaline, I think."

"So, anyway, during that whole 9/11 time-on the initial day-I woke up, went downstairs and saw the chaos, looking downtown. Actually a lot of folks didn't know what had actually happened at first. Downtown Manhattan, where the World Trade Center had been, was just a gray-black cloud and you couldn't see anything. As mentioned, I was living on Morton street, with my room overlooking Sixth Avenue. And there were all these cars stopped on Avenue of the Americas-Sixth Avenue-with their radios playing and trying to get reports of what was happening. It was a strange, surreal scene: all these cars stopped, with their doors open and the car radios all blaring the news simultaneously, up and down the avenue. Never heard anything like it. And people were looking down at the ruinous black cloud and rumoring, giving the strangest, made-up explanations because a lot of them didn't know what was happening, except through hearsay. For example, someone said to me when I asked what had happened, 'A Cesna [light airplane] hit one of the towers, and that tower caught on fire and fell over and hit that other tower and they both fell down...' Or, 'One of the towers fell over, and because they're both connected below ground, the other one fell down as well.'"

"But anyway, my point is, when I went down I was

sharing an office space...I had a small desk space at a place called Organization of Independent Artists down on Hudson Street, about five blocks away from the World Trade Center. I would edit videos there late into the night, and in fact had been up the night before well into the early hours of the morning. My plan was to cut until dawn, then go down to the Marina, next to the World Trade center and get a coffee. But, I went home before then, around 3 or 4 in the morning. Anyway, as a result I woke up after the towers had already collapsed, and had been woken up as I said by the sound of the car radios lined up, blaring on Sixth Avenue."

"So I immediately went down to Hudson Street when I sort of saw something really precipitous and epic was happening downtown. I made it downtown to the art space, as I said, only five blocks from Ground Zero, and it was clear that there was no established order, even amongst the police, the fire department. I mean, they were trying, yes, but it was like a wartime-type situation, and everybody was rushing in...people were staggering out covered in white dust. Some people were walking by completely unscathed and oblivious, with Starbucks cups, you know, cups of coffee in their hands. And they'd be passing this person staggering out of the cloud, covered in white dust, like a zombie. It was just like this mad circus."

"Here's my point. What I'd like to point out, regarding the self-governing society is that people behaved themselves. There was no looting. There was no...or minimal exploitation of the situation. I think a couple delis raised their prices on bottled water, something like that. But people generally were self-governing. So, when push comes to shove, I think society as a whole, when left unregulated, without a big government monitoring it, is not destined to sink into anarchy."

"Which is the ironic thing about Lawrence Ferlinghetti's statement about BookWars. People, without any necessary prompting or conditioning to do so...most-not all-but most will generally adhere to a civil way of functioning. A civil society that functions without significant intervention by a central or local government. Maybe that's the kind of anarchy he's talking about? And that's an insight I gained from selling books on the street. We were unregulated, except near the end when we were forced, you know, to get a tax stamp...which some of us got. Some of the more 'together' of us got it, and some stragglers, the 'super-laissez faire', never got it. But we were still all nonetheless self-regulating. And insofar as the sidewalk booksellers were unregulated externally, they still were self-moderating to a degree and had their own code of ethics which functioned in a workable way within the rest of society. I think that's very telling. That it can work. And so, that would be another key insight that I gained from the whole experience."

"Besides that, yeah, I mean there were many stories and anecdotes and things I learned about people, about human nature. I'm not trying to glorify it all, there were some very tough times, too, times when it was a grind. I mean, that's the reality of bootstrapping your way through: it's not always going to be smooth, or happy, or glamorous. But I did come away with some gems. How folks may have sustained some incredible challenges and bounced back ...maybe they were broke and then they found a way to make a living, maybe selling books or whatever, and they pulled themselves up and that sort of sling-shotted them into a whole new viable way of life."

"Some of the less joyful or celebratory insights might be that, if you are on the street or working in the public forum, whether you're a hot dog man or you're selling fine art work, or hand-made leather bags or whatever, you're still considered by many to be coarse, 'a part of the street.' And there are plenty of people in New York who are kind of, part of the elite echelons who may judge you, and just write you off as some kind of underling, belonging to the street."

"For example, after graduating from NYU film school, even though I was a Trustee Scholar, when I was selling books on the corner of Mercer and West 4th, I frequently saw a woman I knew from film school. We'd been in the same acting class together, got along well at the time, and so forth. And I remember, when I was selling on the street, she would pass by the stand–but she wouldn't stop to say anything. It was as if she had decided to put blinders on because I was, quote unquote, unworthy. Or coarse. Or uncouth. Because I was a component of the street: I had to be invisible, unworthy. Even though I was often raking in hundreds of dollars in cash a day, which was a lot for me at the time, more than I would have made at production work. And I was using that money to push forward with my movie projects, you know, bootstrapping them along any way I could."

I ask the filmmaker how, exactly, this status or class difference may be communicated, if not explicitly or directly.

"I think it's a kind of mind state, or a pheromone-like thing that is exuded unconsciously or not, which folks can pick up on with invisible feelers and thereby evaluate each other. And of course, there are the overt things, visible status symbols and so forth. But a lot of it is transmitted in an apparently 'psychic' or unconscious way. Thus, if you indicate or demonstrate, or project, that you're part of a certain strata or working class, then you may well be pigeonholed or judged by others. You may be judged. I mean, there is a class [system] in America. We all know that now. It's a class society, driven by a small sliver of elites. Not that I agree with this, but that's the way it appears to be. Anyway, I didn't quite realize this until I'd spent time working in the public forum."

"Princeton University, for example, in 2014, conducted and released their famous study...which determined that the United States is not actually a democracy. The report concluded, essentially, that the US today–its policy, its economy– is determined by very narrow range of elites. And you see that there is a schism between the so-called elites–people who have a lot of money, often through their lineage, through inheritance, financial or other assets–and those who are 'not elite' or patrician."

Does Rosette think there's any hope of change?

"I think that's just part of human nature, you know. But it does seem to be out of balance in the USA. The middle class in American must come back or the country will wither fold or descend into a revolutionary condition. On the other hand, the direct alternative would be a sort of socialist situation which...obviously didn't work out. And there's no escaping it, it's human nature, it's universal."

"I've seen it over here in Asia for instance too, yeah, it's very hierarchical. You have the big man–or woman in the case of Myanmar–and the proxies and underlings pyramiding down beneath in a sort of cascade. And you're expected to fit in. I'm talking about locals. As a foreigner, it's slightly different. The foreigner is an alien, never quite fully blending in, nor is there that expectation. The foreigner may be befriended, however, and then displayed as a show of wealth or power–somewhat similar to the posse effect I alluded to earlier regarding my Hollywood colleague in LA."

"But yeah, I also think that would be an insight...despite the rhetoric or the history, or claims to the contrary, that America is definitely a class society. And it was the elites–people with power, as indicated by the Princeton study regarding the state of democracy in

America–who were driving the whole Quality of Life program really, pushing the Mayor and the administration to do something. To clean up the streets. Those influential actors may have been real estate developers, or a university in the neighborhood, or whatnot. Entities with augmented power were at work in an ostensibly pluralistic democratic society, driving–I wouldn't say mandating what happens–but certainly influencing what happened in New York City to a greater than normal degree."

I feel honor bound to the public-at-large to ask whether Rosette learned any dark secrets.

"I'm not sure what you mean, but I don't have any dark secrets, actually. No dark secrets about those times, or that particular occupation. It was generally pretty open along those lines. The way of the bookseller was generally very transparent and pretty open. The whole bookseller environment. By way of example, let's say there was a new bookseller who just had come and set up near you. Unlike many other stratified or hierarchical environments, the street booksellers would usually welcome the stranger and, you know, wouldn't prod or poke them with their elbows and pelt them with various rules but would just let them be. You know, there was no initiation or...there was no hazing, as you can see in other cliques and groups. It was interesting in that respect."

"And let's say by way of example the new bookseller needed to go get a slice of pizza, or take a piss, whatever. It was understood that the neighboring bookseller would watch the table, and if someone bought a book would collect the money, and would hand the money over without any–not even a thought of keeping it. It was beyond a code. It was almost like a holy thing. You would never keep another bookseller's money. That was striking, too. And that all went without being said. It's not like the new bookseller would show up and then there was a pow-wow where everyone sat down and told them the rules and who was in charge, you know the sort of stuff that often goes on with many other workplace environments and subcultures and communities. That didn't happen."

"It was forgiving and loose, and accommodating. Maybe because the booksellers were kind of a common tribe–as a group–dealing with a range of external forces? The weather alone was an external force. So there were many, many instances where the code of the booksellers' society automatically leapt into play almost instinctively without anyone explaining what to do. And that was really insightful."

Does Rosette think self-regulation is a hardwired human attribute?

"Yes, I can see that being a part of human nature. But, it seems like that quality is being threatened these days, as more and more people abrogate their personal power to an external system–willfully or not, consciously or not. And as I mentioned with the 9/11 example, that, when push comes to shove, generally speaking if people are not...are allowed to act on their own critical thinking and initiative, will generally function well without being dicks to each other. And with their own set of reasonable uncodified rules."

"I think it's just a minority of unbalanced persons who cause trouble and put people on edge in society, especially in a litigious society like America. However it has happened over the years, the States seems to have become so litigious and codified I think the sense of normal, reasonable self-regulation has atrophied. I hope it can come back–that's part of the Great America I remember."

12. TRUTH VS. FICTION / SKILLS & THRILLS

Do the skills and techniques a filmmaker employs and learns while producing documentaries carry over into feature films? Or is fictional, scripted narrative an artform that flexes different muscles and offers its own challenges?

"I would say it's an and/or," Rosette begins." I went on after BookWars to make a fiction feature road movie called <u>Lost in New Mexico</u>-made in New Mexico as the name may suggest. That was also a very bootstrap project, my first fiction feature, also made with hardly any money or backing. That's another story, of course, maybe to include somewhere else at another time. And then somewhat later, that being recently-in the past couple years-I made another drama here in Southeast Asia, a fictional supernatural drama called <u>Freedom Deal: Story of Lucky</u>. Freedom Deal is set along the Cambodia-Vietnam border in 1970 during the Vietnam War. I directed that in Khmer [Cambodian] language, which I've learned over the years being in the region. More on that in another discussion too, I reckon."

"Prior to BookWars, my first major effort I had undertaken, besides short films and videos at NYU film school and back in Ohio when I was growing up, was <u>Charlie's Box</u>. Charlie's Box is a psychological drama, shot and produced completely on film, shot in Brooklyn. It was my first indie effort, made shortly after I graduated from NYU. The movie uses a classical approach regarding coverage: I broke down and covered the script with close-ups, medium close-ups, wide shots, etc. It was all storyboarded precisely, with lighting diagrams and notes, proper continuity, and so forth. That was a drama too, as mentioned."

"So, to answer your question: do the skills and techniques employed while making documentaries carry over into feature films? Some of them. Probably, most notably, editing. Enhancing my editing chops. I edited

BookWars nearly completely, for instance, with the assistance at one point of a talented commercial editor in San Francisco named Greg Janza, in order to get another fresh set of eyes on it. Even so, I made most of the edit decisions, cutting on the machine on my own, and just basically showed the cut to the co-producers once in a while for feedback. As a result, I became a much better editor. And my timing as an editor became much better after dealing with all that material-looking at the material, editing it...media management skills. That is, organizing the media. That skill improved too. Naturally that carries over into fiction as well."

I've read, and heard from other filmmakers, that the documentary format often employs a certain amount of fictive elements. Does the filmmaker have any thoughts on this?

"Documentary and fiction...some people uphold a real strict definition, or dividing line, between the two; and I'm not so sure the definition is that clear. I'm more inclined to say that both of them are visual storytelling methods. Just by the nature of setting up a camera, and choosing shots...a lot of documentaries happen to be really fictionalized in many ways, in terms of the selection of subject; the selection of which content appears to form a storyline. I don't believe in pure documentary or pure fiction."

"I believe in visual storytelling. And in that sense, being able to acquire imagery, upload it to the machine and edit, is a universal translatable skill. Obviously with documentary, you should not be prompting or directing subjects or participants to do anything. It's observational, letting the camera roll. And by virtue of letting the camera roll a lot in order to capture the moments you need, Number One: unless you're really flush with cash, you're shooting on digital. And Number Two: you'll end up with a very high shooting ratio–maybe 50 or 100: 1, something like that, which means there's a lot of work done in the editing bay, in the edit."

"Documentaries, the saying goes, are made in the edit room. I would say that's partly true. I would say it's more true, certainly more true, than a classically covered fiction piece. By classically covered I mean, with a fiction film, you start with a script. You develop the script until it's pretty much fine-tuned. Then you cast it, lock it in, and the script is not really supposed to change much at all once production commences–though it often does. And, in the planning stage, you develop a shot list and you plan the coverage of the script. That is, in this sequence, a DP

[Director of Photography] and director might say this is where the close-ups will be...so we'll set up close-ups for these shots, this dialogue, this action. And we'll match the action or overlap that, cover it with medium shots and maybe a wider master shot. That's classical coverage. Do a wide master to cover everything, or a medium shot, then your medium close-ups, your close-ups, your over-the-shoulder, reverse, etc., and then any pick-up lines you need. That's fiction coverage."

"It sounds mechanical and straightforward, but it's not easy. The main challenge with fiction is that you've got to sustain this illusion that, despite possibly shooting on different days, and at different times in different moods of the talent involved, you've got to sustain the illusion of continuity. And that's really the challenge of fiction. Creating the illusion of continuity, where the production was most likely not continuous at all."

"Documentaries are far more forgiving in that sense, in that if you don't have continuity–and you're not expected to, really–if a shot jumps suddenly to something else, it's acceptable by virtue of the medium. It's forgiven. People understanding the genre immediately cut it some slack and say, 'well, this is reality, so it's allowed to jump around.' Whereas fiction is not permitted to jump around, generally speaking, if you're assembling a continuous sequence. So I would say, having worked in both formats, I would say narrative fiction is more demanding than documentary on that technical side."

"On the other hand, documentaries still require their own particular skills set and technique...it's a different sensibility. You may be hunting for material over time, and everything that goes along with that is part of the game. You may be shooting on your own, or often are shooting on your own or with a small crew on a documentary, so you need to be able to shoot, to operate the gear, to frame shots, to expose decently, and to do this on your own unless you have a dedicated DP. You need to be able to set up shots, have an eye for material, to predict what might happen...you kind of gain a sixth sense about what participants-people in the documentary-might or might not do. You develop a kind of a "Spidey sense" about when to continue sticking around, when to keep shooting, when more material might be forthcoming. So it's more of an intuition, in terms of shooting a documentary, versus fiction narrative. I'm talking about classically covered fiction where it's got to be planned out more thoroughly."

The two forms-fiction and nonfiction-share certain

skill sets. Do the limitations inherent to a crime thriller, or drama, make them more difficult to pull off?

"I would say the two forms share an editing skill set, for sure. And then there's the other technical side, the mix. Color correction? Well, not all documentaries do as thorough of a color correction, or grading, as fiction. The score...probably the score, the composition, the soundtrack–is probably more developed in fiction, but not always. Just as a ballpark figure, I would say shooting fiction with planned coverage and matching action and continuity, is more challenging, planning-wise at least. And I would say by a factor of at least two to three, if not more. A lot of emerging filmmakers start with documentaries, because the form is more forgiving. I'm not belittling documentaries, I'm talking about the costs of adhering to the requirements of the fiction format."

"Let's say, for example, you're shooting a scene at night, but it's supposed to take place in the morning because of your script, because of the story. You've got to be able to set up lights or have a gaffer, or a DP and gaffer and electrician–and crew–you know, the grips and so forth, set up the lights to match the morning look that you had before. You've also got a script person doing continuity. Technically speaking, if you're seeking to maintain some illusion of continuity, then the requirements of the fiction form are a lot less forgiving than in documentaries."

"With that being said, there are certain filmmakers doing fiction in completely alternative or experimental ways, where the conventions of the medium do not demand that kind of consistency. If you look at an unusual fiction classic, such as Godard's Alphaville [1965], that's technically a fiction film. But there's very little matching action, very little classical coverage. It's almost like an experimental film. So, continuity is–I haven't seen that movie in a while by the way, correct me if I'm wrong–it's not as rigorous as it would be in a, let's say, a classically covered movie, such as a movie by Hitchcock, or most contemporary Hollywood dramas with traditional dialogue scenes and so forth. Dialogue scenes where you've got to match words, you've got to match eyelines, you've got to match the axis of the camera and so forth."

"Then again, some filmmakers work in multiple areas. Take, for instance, Werner Herzog, who works in documentaries and fiction–pretty successfully actually–or has. Directs operas too, apparently. If you look at **Aguirre, the Wrath of God [1972], it does have some classical fiction** coverage. Yet, it primarily has a documentary-type feeling. I mean, if you look at the end of Aguirre on the barge...they're floating down that jungle barge...even though it's a very loose fiction film, the filmmakers still have some continuity to deal with because of the monkeys that are there on the barge. That is, they must have to wrangle the monkeys between shots, regather them, whatnot, restage them for the subsequent coverage. So even there, in that scene at least, they've got to work with some degree of continuity. I imagine they had to, after each shot, stop the barge or do something to halt its progress while they set up the next shot."

"But, that movie is a little looser. It's not quite as continuous as your blue-chip Hollywood film. Even a hyper-kinetic Hollywood movie like Mad Max: Fury Road is largely linear and continuous. A movie like Twelve Monkeys, considerably less so, and more 'quantum-like.' But take another nontraditional fiction movie like Performance [1970], by Nicolas Roeg and Donald Cammell–his co-director, you know, with Mick Jagger. That movie's very experimental, but it's technically fiction. Yet there's a lot of jump cuts, continuity is not really required so rigorously, because the filmic language established by the filmmakers doesn't demand it."

"Or take another nontraditional fiction film, like Gummo. Same thing. I suppose, then, that's the decisive factor: if you set up a movie to be less rigorously continuous for the audience, even if it's fiction–if you set that up clearly and establish that to the audience, then they will be forgiving. Because you've telegraphed the rules to them initially, so they can 'float' with the style and approach the director has established."

"Continuing on with transferable skill sets...another skill set that transfers over between the fiction and documentary worlds would be part of the producing skill set. Pitching, presenting, and persuading. And fundraising, including crowdfunding, if you are attempting to raise a budget that way. Crowdfunding was in a very primitive form when I did BookWars back in the late 1990s. I was basically doing the crowdfunding manually, via hard copy and one-sheets being sent out, or emails to a target group of potential contributors...then having people send contributions to your fiscal sponsor or PayPal account or whatever."

"Now, of course, crowdfunding–Kickstarter, Indiegogo, and all the others...they're huge. We crowdfunded on IndieGogo for our recent supernatural Asian drama, Freedom Deal: Story of Lucky, which we shot on location in Cambodia. My filmmaker aka for that one was 'Jack RO.' As mentioned, folks can watch that one on Amazon Video and elsewhere–it's actually a medium length drama designed to develop an expanded feature version. But that movie, and my decade long experiences in Asia, are another story altogether."

"In the end, your abilities to pitch a project, support the project, persuade people to come on board...all of those transfer over from documentary to fiction and back to documentary as well. The ability to pitch and persuade–that's universal to any field a bootstrapper may be working in, whatever the industry or business. I mean, that's more of a character thing. I mean character in terms of the character of the producer, or the primary driver of the project. So everything you learn from pitching and producing and pushing a project to completion, whether it's documentary or fiction, will empower you for working in other forms and genres, if that should be the case."

13. SHOWDOWN / THE OTHER ELVIS / DUST-UP!

During BookWars' production, another group was in progress writing a book about New York City street booksellers, and a major publisher–Farrar, Straus and Giroux–had commissioned their work. BookWars, in their eyes, appeared to be an existential threat.

One individual associated with that other project went so far as to engage in psychological warfare, making email statements vowing to distribute anti-BookWars flyers to participants in the movie to persuade them not to participate in the movie's production. Were that to happen today, Twitter would be blazing! How did Rosette first learn of this antipathy? Were the threatened flyers actually handed out? And how does a bootstrap project manager handle unexpected, destructive curve balls like this?

"Well, I do recall the beginning. I remember going to NYU and hanging up some flyers on the graduate film floor. I think that was the tenth floor, at 721 Broadway, at my old film school, though I'd gone there as an undergrad down on the ninth floor. Anyway, I was interested in screening a cut of BookWars to get feedback. I was attempting to wrangle a fine cut screening, something like that. So I had hung up these flyers, with my email address. Some days later, a couple days later, I got an email back from a guy who I thought was of Middle Eastern origin. Hus name was 'Hakim Hasan.' Anyway, in the email he said something to the effect of: 'I have learned about this movie you're making about street booksellers. This is certainly an important development and I would like to see the film right away. Hakim Hasan.'

"And my first thought was, hmm, I don't have a huge team, and I'm not really able to do individual screenings. I wanted to do a group screening, like a focus group. So I replied to him and said that I wouldn't be able to provide an individual screening for him, I don't have the exact words here, but it was civil enough. Pretty matter of fact and straight forward, definitely not over the top, saying that when we do a public screening, whether that's a work-in-progress screening or a fine cut screening or a festival release, I'll be sure to let him know.

"And from that point on it escalated. This guy became very hardcore, very angry, very antagonistic, and set out to interfere with the production of BookWars as if his life depended on it. I didn't know at that time he was involved with that other project, a sociology book called Sidewalk being written by a professor whom I met several times when I was out there. Mitch–Mitchell Duneier, the professor–was civil and affable, at least in person. I don't know how things were operating below the line. But really in terms of the direct action, and the overt interference, that came from the other fellow, Hakim, who was the key participant in their book."

Rosette forwarded me a number of the archived emails; these gave me an unsettling glimpse into a hidden world behind the process of the bootstrapping-filmmaker.

"When I looked at these emails again in preparation for this book, I actually felt sympathy for this guy. I don't feel like sharing the more extreme stuff, but will provide a few snippets here as sort of historical reference material. He's otherwise quite eloquent. It turns out, though, in terms of his backstory, he apparently was fired from a job some time ago and he cited as a reason for this his race. The employer was white. And he, Hakim, is a person of color. He was sure it was a race issue, racial profiling, and apparently since that time he had an ax to grind."

The filmmaker read me a few excerpts from the emails; there is a surreal quality in hearing Rosette 'condemn' himself as he reads from the original emails:

"'You did, in fact, place beer in the hand(s) of one of the vendors on Sixth Avenue* and, Jason, if I were you, I would simply leave this alone; otherwise, the evidence is going to be brought forth.'

"Here, he's accused me of forcibly placing beer in the hands of the [mainly African and Caribbean American] Sixth Avenue booksellers so I could show them getting drunk. Incredible, and totally out of the blue. What would be my motivation–to show their so called 'inferiority'? And how do you 'place beer' into someone's hand? Do you unwrap their fingers and then wrap their fingers back around the can or bottle? I don't get it. The ironic thing is, I actually depicted the booksellers on W4th street getting drinking, actively getting drunk, not the booksellers on 6th avenue. It's right there in the movie–anyone can see it."

The filmmaker continues reading another of the unsolicited emails:

"'Dear Jason: Quite frankly, judging from you and your film, I don't think you have the mental acumen to discern what my role on Sixth Avenue, let alone what Jane Jacobs it leads to–in theoretical terms–as a public character. You're way out of your league here, and there's no evidence in your film that you even remotely understand what you're talking about. For the record, Ron asked me many years ago if I would be willing to participate in your film and I declined, and for good reason.'"

Rosette breaks off suddenly. "I have no clue what he was talking about there. I only arrived back in New York a few months prior, to do some pickup shooting and to finish the movie, and I hadn't met Ron yet."

"'You're not intcrested in depicting black people in your film who are capable of thinking. Nor are you willing to acknowledge that there's a variation in experience that existed when I worked on Sixth Avenue. So if being a thinking person makes me self-absorbed, I am guilty as charged. Let me get to the point. For years you have passed yourself off as some kind of expert on bookselling on the street.'

"He comes right out with it here and throws the 'race card' at me, at our project. That's really not justified. But there's something else behind this. There's more to this all than meets the eye."

Rosette reads some more: "'I regard you as a two-bit hustler masquerading as a filmmaker. Nothing more, nothing less.'"

"Two-bit hustler...lots of anger, but, I never even met the guy. Here, he refers to an article written in Publishers Weekly. The title is 'Taking It to the Streets,' [published in issue #27: July 3, 2000] written by John High. Mr. High refers to both of our projects in this column, in this story."

"...'I was appalled when I read John High's article, "Taking It to the Streets," in Publishers Weekly. I called Mr. High's office Friday afternoon. I'm requesting a meeting with the editor-in-chief of Publishers Weekly and asking for space to respond to what I see as the racist subtext of his article.'

"Anyone can go ahead and Google this article, 'Taking it to the Streets'", Rosette says. "It's not a racist article. It's a pretty well-written and balanced overview of both our projects, I think."

Rosette reads some more, his voice coming flatly and with a more resigned tone out of my computer speakers. It sounds as if he's reading a courtroom transcript:

"'I tried to give you free advice last summer, and you failed to listen. I haven't the slightest idea what Mr. High is talking about in my case. I am not a refugee from corporate America. I was fired from my position as a legal proofreader at the law firm of Robinson-Silverman over eight years ago. I believe the basis of my termination was racially motivated.'

"And that must be the basis of his anger," comments Rosette.

"...'I wrote about this in my Afterword to Sidewalk, an excerpt of which was published in The New York Times Magazine.'

"And you can see his link with The New York Times. He had some contacts there."

The filmmaker continues reading, dutifully voicing

words that had been launched against him:" 'Some of these men had drug problems'–he's talking to me about the guys on Sixth Avenue–'and when you were not trying to put beer in their hands so you could film them drinking, you were busy trying to film them for nothing.'"

Rosette clarifies the accusations that the men were exploited and not compensated:

"First of all, as mentioned, I never 'placed beer in their hands'–that's ludicrous and bizarre. Secondly, you're not supposed to pay participants in documentaries, and I didn't generally. I did actually end up giving some money to Ron just because by this time Hakim had interfered so thoroughly I had no choice. But you're actually not supposed to pay participants. It was a forum for them to articulate what they felt about their experience. And they understood that and they agreed. Obviously I'm not making big bucks from the movie since I'm still paying it off fifteen years later."

"I was–try to understand–I was just trying to put this movie together. Trying to protect the project. It took a tremendous effort and sacrifice to get this movie made, bootstrapping the project without any safety net, which I think anyone can discern here. And this guy comes along and states that he was going to hand out flyers to all the guys on Sixth Avenue [telling them] not to participate in our movie project. Well, there's another lesson for anyone who's bootstrapping a project–you have to be ready to handle anything that may come along."

Reading deeper into Hakim's messages to Rosette is daunting and somewhat disturbing, considering the director's above comments. How Hasan came to be associated with the sociology project, Sidewalk–and writing the Afterword–remains inexplicable to me. Did Rosette receive any support from his New York producer?

"The co-producer in New York, Michel Negroponte, was not either disposed or inclined, or able to, you know, use elbows to push these guys away. He may have been concerned for his reputation, and so remained aloof. I mean, a producer...there are different styles and types. Michel was not, you know, a 'hardball' producer. He was more into the aesthetics of the documentary format, and was offering suggestions and advice, and some referrals, but he was mainly more like a coach. I don't believe he had much experience really bootstrapping a project in that way, which, as can be seen here, isn't always an even or pretty process. Even so, some diplomatic intervention would have been welcome. He was the only key point person the project had in New York. But it was not forthcoming, and that was somewhat disappointing at the time."

"Putting two-and-two together later, circumstantially, it was evident that this guy Hakim–through his connections at The New York Times, as he had just written something in advance for the book project he was working on which appeared in the Times–had made contact with Elvis Mitchell, who was then a Times movie reviewer."

"Elvis Mitchell was a movie reviewer for The Times, and is a person of color, and a supporter and defender of people of color, African-American filmmakers, and so forth. Based on Hakim's previous behavior and statements thus far, our project had been portrayed to that reviewer as a racist document, which obviously would not then encourage a positive review under those circumstances."

"So they pulled some strings and tried to torpedo our project. They saw BookWars as a rival or existential threat, though it wasn't, it was just a parallel project with modest overlap. True, though, by that point they were also working on a video documentary to support their book.

And they had a lot of backing from a massive publisher, Farrar Strauss, Giroux, so they would have the physical resources to try to extinguish any undesirable project. That's hardball-but that's life. It's a very valuable learning experience in any case-anything goes. It's asymmetrical, yes, but I've since learned there are ways to counter that sort of thing, even with limited resources."

"Aside from any friction between parallel projects, one of their key participants had sustained some kind of attack or slight in his life which he perceived to be racially motivated. The project I was working on, myself included, thus became a mobilizing foil for that as well. The result is what you can see in the New York Times review of BookWars. It was quite a misinformed and negative review, and it was a complete anomaly in that it followed all the other very positive earlier reviews of the movie. But that's life-things are at times perceived to be a zero-sum game, and this was an attempt to knock the legs out from under our project. I think the ultimate loser, though, was the public forum of New York City, which could have used as many championing documents, such as BookWars, and including Sidewalk, for that matter, to help keep the public forum public."

"I don't know to what degree, if at all, the professor

writing the book, Mitch Duneier, was involved in what was going on. But again, he and his key participant Hakim had been working very closely together for a long time and they were in thorough and constant communication."

"It did have a stunting effect on our distribution efforts for a while. But then the movie grew legs again and kept going, and once again gained mainly positive reviews after that. Kevin Thomas and the LA Times, the New Yorker, they were all positive. So any critical thinker can put two-and-two together and determine what had been going on behind the scenes, given all the uninvited interference and foment that occurred."

"Incidentally, there was another person who seemed to be part of the equation, but he was slightly more behind the scenes and I never met him or communicated with him directly. As mentioned, part of their overall book project involved the making of a video documentary of the scenario to support the book, a documentary of the environment of the Sixth Avenue booksellers."

"Now, the guy shooting the video for them was a fellow named Barry Brown. And Barry Brown, who I never met, was usually known as Barry Brown, comma, Spike

Lee's editor. It was never just 'Barry Brown.' It was always, 'Barry Brown, comma, Spike Lee's editor, was here.' Or, 'Barry Brown, comma, Spike Lee's editor, was asking about BookWars.' And so forth."

"So, slowly, from that side, more and more feelers were being extended toward BookWars as I was bootstrapping and straining to complete the project, and there was basically a constant probing coming from that particular direction to see what we were doing, what I was doing. It made me feel uncomfortable. So finally I told them as much. I don't recall flipping out or being a dick, just stating that I wanted to be left alone to complete my project."

"It was around that time that Michel-the New York co-producer, Michel Negroponte-calls and says, 'You know, I've had a discussion with Barry Brown, comma, Spike Lee's editor, who's working with so and so...and he said that there's some discord. Or something, like that, I don't remember the exact words."

"Anyway, Michel said, 'I heard that you've had some issues with so and so, and the other project. And I'm going to have to step away from BookWars.' That development was unfortunate, because Michel was basically the key producerly point person for the movie in New York. On the instructional side of things, however, and this should be noted by any bootstrappers out there: this was an interesting and classic indicator of a mobbing effort. Go ahead and Google 'mobbing' if you don't know what it is.'"

"Mobbing, it turns out, is a common phenomenon in the entertainment industry, for a range of reasons. It's common in a smaller sector with a very elastic economic base. Basically, mobbing involves a concentrated group attack against a single individual, or target, which has been marked as a potential intruder by an existing Alpha in the territory-a potentially intruding rival. It has its roots in animal group behavior, but any human organization or community may exhibit these traits as well. When a target is being mobbed, friends and allies will often peel off and disappear to avoid becoming a target themselves. The downside of this is that the target remains further exposed without essential allies to assist. In our case, Michel would ultimately come back around later again as we got closer to completion, when screenings and press started to happen. At that point, some folks congratulated him on 'his film'-ironic and surreal, but that's the movie world for you."

"In the meantime, I did my best to drive the project forward on my own, while trying to deal with the interference as best I could."

I mention that this level of interference, without much moral support, must have felt like a bad play in the Absurdist tradition.

"It was absurd, and completely unexpected. At times I did wonder if it would have been best to just stay on the West coast and release the movie at 90% completion. I mean, I had a good job there at last, a girlfriend, and the movie was substantially complete. Why bother dealing with the negative financial impact and hassle of leaving a steady job to head back East, only to deal with that stuff on the home stretch?"

"I also wonder why they [the team involved with Sidewalk] just didn't approach me directly to cut a deal. Something along the lines of 'Hey, we'd like to have exclusivity in this area, can we work something out?' Maybe we could have hashed things out and settled on something, who knows."

"Anyway, at a certain point you have to set your boundaries. I was the scrappy, independent, grass roots, bootstrapping filmmaker, and I was really having to fend for myself and finish this project. At one point, I did outreach directly to Mitch, who was the sociologist authoring the book whose participant had undertaken the negative outreach. I emailed him when it was really getting out of hand. I said, 'Mitch, you know, Hakim is...he's out of control. Can you lean on him and ask him to stop?' Something like that."

"But Mitch declined. He just replied: 'Hakim is his own man.'

"So, I guess there are lessons to be learned from that. One of them would be to make sure your team-project manager, producer, editor, whatnot-that they are either your very, very best friends with absolute loyalty, or they have 'skin in the game.' Money or assets invested, that is. Make sure that they have a real, hardcore interest in making sure the project is defended and completed successfully."

"Now with all that being said, I'm not saying that I'm the perfect diplomat, or I'm, you know, completely faultless...we're all human beings. But I can tell you it's very, very challenging to be as bland and affable and diplomatic as everyone would like after going through hell to scrape together and bootstrap to complete a project under circumstances like that."

"The lesson of all that interference is, as far as I can discern: Number One, try to survey the territory as closely as you can, or get some discerning eyeballs on the ground, to survey the territory to see who may be out there doing a similar project. And try to assess whether they are friendly, or whether they might consider your project to be an existential threat. I mean, there's always some rivalry to some degree between similar or overlapping projects. Sometimes it's friendly rivalry, sometimes it's an uneasy rivalry; sometimes it's just a cool sort of standoffish thing. In my case, it was very hot. That would be one lesson, I guess. Try to survey the territory and make an assessment of who the stakeholders and gatekeepers are."

"The next lesson would be: you need to have a producer, or other key team member, who's got elbow, and who's willing to use them. It's not enough, I think, to just have connections and have an aesthetic sensibility and whatnot. You need somebody who's got elbows–someone else, besides yourself–standing by in the event some trouble comes along so they can defend the project space. Let's face it, despite the rhetoric and grooming, even the most cultivated society still seems to be basically ape-like, beneath the surface. Whether in the office or in the movie making world, there are Alpha leaders, submissive underlings, and suspected intruders who may be perceived as a rival or threat. So someone is needed to defend the project at all costs, someone with elbows, besides the maker-creator who may be completely occupied; or, at the very least, that stakeholder can promote a diplomatic intervention and constructive meeting between all parties."

"The last major lesson that I gather from this–it's kind of laughable, and it may sound funny, but it's true I think, and it's also very challenging if it's not your natural disposition. It's this: you have to try and be bland and affable, and smooth and nice at times, even as you may be clawing away to complete or even defend your project. These days especially, where everyone seems to be offended by something, you have to try to be as bland and affable as possible, no matter how tough things are or hard you're red-lining it budget-wise."

"Even if, by the end of the project, you're exhausted and living on a friend's couch, like I was. Near the end of the process of making BookWars, for instance, by the time it was nearly finished in New York, I was gasping, dazed. Moaning like a zombie. I was pouring all of my remaining money into the audio mix and making the broadcast masters and the M&E (international) version of the movie. A couple thousand dollars, burnt and blasted...spent, gone. So, as alluded to, I was sharing a couch with this friendly, overweight cat named 'Petey.' It was Rick's cat, belonging to 'Slick' Rick–one of the street booksellers from BookWars."

"I was staying at Rick's place on Houston street, trying to stave off the need to use any of the remaining advance money from the Arte/ZDF sale on renting a room or apartment, because I needed to make sure I completed the deliverables for the movie. And Rick was going through a rough time himself. The environment was hairy (literally), strewn with Rick's books, papers, whatnot. The cat hair on the couch grew thicker and gradually formed itself into a sort of carpet, like a hair piece. I'd sometimes find part of it upon my head in the morning. So there I was, living on the couch with Petey the cat, watching thousands of dollars from the Arte/ZDF advance money get poured into doing the mix, the color correction, etcetera, instead of going towards a lease, a place to rent."

"But there was nothing else I could do. It was the only way. I had no folks in New York. I had been staying in the small studio where I had been editing, but that was all wrapped up. So it was the couch with Petey the cat or nothing. That is bootstrapping–doing whatever is necessary to fulfill the mission. I didn't have a car to sleep in at that point. But at least I had a roof over my head and wasn't homeless, I'm grateful for that and I give thanks to Rick and Beth for helping out in that way. If you have a wolf by the ears, you can't let it go. You have to keep going and hold on until you put it away, put the project away."

"Anyway, living in marginal, red-line environments like that for an extended period of time, bootstrapping and clawing away to move forward with a project, will not likely result in you being bland and affable. But the paradox is: you have to be bland and affable to function well in the independent filmmaking world, or other similarly small community resting on an elastic economy, lest you set off social landmines. The exception would be if you've established yourself and you're so unassailably 'big' that you can more or less speak your mind."

"In that case, you would have achieved an Alpha state and your underlings can swoop out to defend you, if desired, by dealing with any offending target for you. But if you're still emerging, still establishing yourself, I would say you have to try to be as bland and affable as possible so as not to offend people. These days at least, where folks seem to be on edge a lot and quite sensitive to things. Anyway, balancing all that was a tremendous challenge for me."

I comment that today's environment is a different universe compared to that of the 1960s and 70s, which were populated by a handful of steely, leather-lunged filmmakers.

The filmmaker responds."That does seem to be the case. Now, looking back on films of the Seventies, you hear legendary stories of people like Sam Peckinpah and whatnot, you know, slugging people, with fights breaking out, and all that. I'm not advising that behavior either...but it's notable that nowadays it seems as though if you just step on the wrong crack, or look at someone the wrong way or say something the wrong way, then all hell breaks loose. It's as if nowadays everybody is offended by something."

"And I think the smaller the community you're working in-the tighter it becomes, and the less slack, it seems-the more likely you are to rub someone the wrong way, especially if you don't identify all the gatekeepers and supplicate yourself to them properly. Especially if you are a newcomer to the territory or sector, in which case you may be perceived as a potential intruder. As mentioned before, this can precipitate a mobbing incident."

"In the animal kingdom, a newcomer who raises red flags amongst the Alphas (the gatekeepers) must roll over and expose its genitals and belly to the Alphas immediately as a sign of submission, or be prepared to fight, or run away. There are only those three options available. But none of those behaviors were really on my radar at the time–I was too focused on finishing my project. So that would be my advice to anyone who finds themselves in a similar boat, whether in an office environment, academic environment, or the indie film world. Just focus on the goal with laser-like intensity and block out any psychological distractions."

"The bootstrapper can have no time for distractions."

I mention that it has been stated in discussions like this, that movies can be defined as merely another commodity. If that should be the case, if movies are commodities–how necessary are they?

"You know, when you look at motion pictures as an economic sector, it's easy to conclude they're not really an absolutely essential commodity. If people didn't have movies...they would go to a concert or go play video games, or whatnot. There are people who would kill me for saying this, for popping that ideological bubble, but it's true, despite the dramatic proclamations. I've spent a lot of time in developing countries and disadvantaged environments. The only essential commodities, really, are clean drinking water, shelter, and food and then, you know-it goes on down from there to education, sanitation, and whatnot."

"Visual storytelling needs can be fulfilled in other ways, including gaming-the gaming sector's huge-theater, reading, and so forth. In ancient times it was the shadow theater, shadow puppets. Flickering lights from a fire inside a cave. Anyway, I think because movies are not an absolutely essential commodity, these days at least, people involved in the sector are rather protective of their territory. The consumer demand is very elastic, with ample opportunities for substitution via other forms of entertainment or diversion."

"So, any newcomer who comes into the sector-the territory-may be perceived as a threat, and could be subject to severe hazing or scrutiny, or even mobbing. We talked about mobbing earlier."

I admit that I'm still not completely familiar with the term.

"Mobbing is...it's like the cousin of bullying. Unlike bullying, it's when a group takes on a target-individual because the target-individual is deemed to be a potential rival to the existing Alpha and the affiliated posse. And this all comes down to the animal kingdom, really. In the animal kingdom, mobbing occurs frequently when an intruder enters the established territory of the Alpha. And the Alpha is usually surrounded, or is surrounded, by a posse of proxies or subindividuals. We talked about the posse effect earlier, when I went out to L.A., and I mentioned my friend there who is an aspiring Alpha wanted me out there to augment his posse. I didn't realize that was why I was invited to go out there at the time."

"Anyway, the interference sustained during the final phases of production of BookWars in New York bore all the hallmarks. It was sparked by an Alpha-or an aspiring proxy to the Alpha-operating in the territory who viewed our project as a potential threat."

"Now, in the animal kingdom, the intruder, or target, has basically three options. The target can supplicate itself, can roll over on its back and expose its genitals and belly to the leader, the rival Alpha. And this is a sign–a clear sign–of submission, which means one has submitted to the other Alpha and that one is not a threat. I guess it takes its different forms in the art and media world...I'm trying to think of what form this might take, the metaphorical rolling over and exposing one's belly and balls: Gushing praise? Throwing a party to honor the Alpha? I dunno'."

"The next option for the target is to leave the territory. The intruder can leave, having been driven out by the Alpha and its team."

"With BookWars, however, I couldn't leave the territory, because I needed to finish the movie, finish the project. I suppose if it had gotten physically violent or, you know, my life was literally at stake–yeah, I could have gotten on a plane or bus and left. It was psychologically violent I guess–the negative inputs from the participant in the book project, the manipulated review in the New York Times, stuff like that. But it wasn't at a physically violent point. It was at the level where, to use an example from the animal kingdom, the lone crow is getting pecked and irritated by the existing community which hopes that he, the intruder becomes increasingly uncomfortable and leaves without any fight."

"In my case, I didn't leave, because I needed to complete the project, not only for myself, but by that point I had to fulfill my fiduciary responsibilities to Arte/ZDF and other broadcasters as well vis-a-vis the deliverables I'd promised."

I recalled that there was a third option-the filmmaker had mentioned, but he had only mentioned two so far.

"The third and final option is that the newcomer-the target, or the intruder-decides to take on, or enter into a contest with the existing Alpha, and prevails."

I considered for a moment: how can someone prevail against an Alpha in that particular situation?

"With BookWars, as mentioned, there was a bit of a dust-up as can be seen from all the emails from the textbook project, from that key participant, all the flyers and disinformation handed out, and the other interventions undertaken to negatively impact our movie. Which again, bears all the hallmarks of a mobbing effort. Now, given the available resources of the other project, versus BookWars-remember, they were fully financed by a major publisher, while I had only a thousand dollar grant from the Playboy Foundation and a modest advance from a European broadcaster-I prevailed to some degree just by sustaining and delivering my completed film."

"I prevailed insofar as I was able to finish the movie. But in my case I had no option. My back was to the wall and I had to press on, or lose everything I'd put into the project. And that wasn't going to happen. I had to keep going, regardless of what local producerly support had changed. That is a key part of the bootstrapping mentality, I think: the show must go on."

"The main reason I'm mentioning that stuff now, looking back and recalling this all, is because I think perhaps useful, in a practical way, for other bootstrapping project managers–whether they be emerging filmmakers, creatives, or other entrepreneurs–to witness as a sort of 'case study' how things actually can work from an inside point of view. Though I would hope this is not a template for anyone."

"Incidentally, I've never met Elvis Mitchell, the reviewer from the Times. When I first heard his name, I didn't know he was a person of color, I just thought of 'Elvis Costello' for some reason and that was the image of him I had in my mind. Elvis Mitchell left the New York Times since then–I'm not sure under what circumstances. I heard that he was busted in 2008 for smuggling cash across the US-Canada border, and he was fired from Roger Ebert's show At the Movies. Then, a bit later, he was let go from the Movieline blog for actually fabricating a review."

I think Rosette makes a very sharp point by mentioning most of the reviews for BookWars were basically positive.

"Anyone can watch the movie and can judge for themselves. Get it on iTunes, on Steam, on Amazon, and it's on some other platforms. But as you're watching, ask yourself: did we disparage, push down, or diminish, the people of color on Sixth Avenue through their portrayal in this movie? Or, did we offer a fair and even mouthpiece, a vehicle for them to share and express their point of view?"

"I think BookWars was absolutely beneficial overall–for them, and for the overall culture of the public forum in New York, the arts in New York City. Which, by the way, is now apparently on the wane. You know, there are all these articles now about how artists are leaving New York due to rising costs and so forth–go ahead and Google it, see what you come up with. It's too bad: our movie was pro-Culture, pro-Public Forum, and pro-New York."

"One note of interest, one final curiosity, is that just

recently I came across the video that Barry Brown had shot and finally completed in support of Mitch's textbook project. I stumbled upon it on YouTube recently. And it says in the credits, it says effectively, '...by the end of his project Mitchell Duneier had become a street bookseller himself.' Maybe not the exact words, something to that effect which you can see on the intro credits."

"Anyway, I was just astonished when I saw that in their movie. It's just factually untrue. I can only guess Mitch, the professor who wrote the book, was drawn in to such a degree that in the end he wanted to actually become what he had been studying. I mean, he wasn't a street bookseller at all; yet that is what his team had finally presented. It could be that he succumbed to the tension between Apollonian and Dionysian forms. That is, the tension or division between being an observing researcher and the participant life of the sidewalk bookseller. Getting the books, hustling to find them, haggling with customers, having discussions with them, being a pivot point in the life of the city-a Dionysian role or position, especially the public forum component. I'm referring, of course, to Nietzsche's Birth of Tragedy."

"Anyway, maybe this testimony, this telling of my experiences back then-the behind the scenes nuts and bolts bootstrapping of a feature movie without any funding or equipment, and all the impossible, improbable effort that went into it–maybe that is actually the point of the whole effort."

"And that everything else, including the movie itself, was just a prologue to a prologue?"

14. THE CAFÉ OF THE OUTSIDE / TV, FESTIVALS & THE WORLD BEYOND

Taking a Best Documentary Award at its festival premiere, plus many positive reviews, had to have been a powerful antidote against Rosette's struggles and tribulations. Given its fraught creation, did the film receive the sort of attention he imagined, or was his intention to get it produced and let the chips fall where they may?

"It was more like this. I may have alluded to this earlier. It was more like pushing the movie as hard as I could to the next step, and then regrouping, usually exhaustedly. It was really tough to make this movie, and looking back, for health and sanity reason, I really flew too close to the sun on that one. No money, no equipment, not even my own camera! It was tough primarily because, looking back on it, in the late 1990s and 2000, the technology was not available like it is now, so I had to actually physically go to where machines were available to edit. Because it's a documentary, the editing component was vitally important. And there was no money, as mentioned. Despite the search for grants, my primitive attempts at fundraising in the pre-crowdfunding days, I was selling books on the streets of New York to get by in between freelance gigs during my very earliest stage of shooting. Obviously I wasn't living large."

"So, by the time I had finished–and I remember this–by the time I finished the last voiceover...I was like a floating, ascending ember–completely and fully burnt up, and burnt out. I remember doing the final voiceover in the movie where the narrator says: 'This is the café of the outside.' I remember doing that VO with a decently jerry-rigged VO setup in the little Upper West Side studio where I was editing, and where I was also staying; I had been doing voiceovers here and there when I could, had some training, and still do them occasionally."

"This was up where the editing machine was at the time in New York–a machine which I was renting, by the way. It wasn't just given to me. I rented it from a couple of documentary filmmakers who had a partnership–Doug Block and Deborah Rosenberg. I paid Doug for the rental.

I never saw him, though, throughout the editing process, since he wasn't involved besides the half-rental of the machine. I offered to pay Deborah-she declined. I considered that a contribution to the movie, which was very much appreciated."

"So, anyway, there I was in that studio in the Upper West Side. I had a voiceover rig set up with some homemade pop filters covering the mics. Pop filters are things that prevent the plosives from spoken words from overcoming the microphone, for example, if you say the word 'Peach,' that first P is a plosive and could cause a pop in the mic, which would ruin the take. My budget was limited, so I had homemade pop filters stretched over clothes hangers which I'd bent into loops...a clothes hanger on the microphone with pantyhose stretched over it. Not my own pantyhose, of course. I stopped wearing those long ago-just kidding. Anyway, yes, and old DIY trick, I just used a couple layers of pantyhose stretched over the bent coat hangers, and that's the pop filter I used for the narration of BookWars. It worked fine. Looked strange to some, sexy to others, but it worked!"

"So that gives you an idea about the process and the nonexistent budget...it was just clawing, clawing, clawing, for about four years. Clawing, clawing, bootstrapping, emailing, clawing, clawing, clawing away. There was no funding. You can see a homemade windscreen in some shots in the movie, too, now that I think of it. Just the very edge of it, made out of wads of cotton tucked together and rubber banded around the mic on the camera. I remember Paul, one of the booksellers who appears in the film, saying one day-'hey it looks like Peter Cottontail's ass!' Peter Cottontail-that's a rabbit from a kid's story right? Though you never know, we were selling books in the Village, and anything goes."

"Oh yes–so, at the very end I remember, when doing that voiceover, 'This is the café of the outside,' I remember I felt like a part of my soul fly away. It lifted up and out, and curled away like a wisp of smoke. I felt it lift out of my body. And float away. I'm not a psychic-type person, either; I'm not a New Age-y person. But I felt it detach, and lift away and float off. As if a part of myself had been burnt up, fully and completely.

"And that, that moment, was the end of the making of the movie. It was like I had staggered across a finish line. It was finally over. The production part at least was over, the editing. The making of the work was complete. But then came the exhibition and distribution component-gads, a whole new effort! Again and again: you have to be prepared to go the limit, push 'til you're gone, and then somehow regather yourself for an entirely new stage. At least that's the way it was for me, with this project, doing it without much support, the only way it could have been done. It wasn't pleasant or fun anymore, but for the sake of the project–I just had to keep going."

"I had kept my eye on distribution, a bit, through the process. There was no talk of distribution from any of the producers, really, leading up to that. No preparatory remarks or formal plan or research from either the Montoya brothers or Michel in New York. Up to the very point of completion, it was really just getting the project done first and foremost."

"So now that the movie is done, obviously it comes time to start to send it out to festivals and events, fine cut events, whatnot, to get exposure. And of course, to sell it. By the way, looking back, it seems like an utterly backwards business model, doing things that way, which was all the 'indie rage' back at the time, and is still apparently used as an approach today."

"That is, producing a product on spec–in this case, a movie-sustaining the entire cost and risk burden, and then trying to sell and market it afterwards, after all the risk has been sustained already and money spent on speculation. It's called a 'Negative Pickup'. Luckily, I did make some decent sales with BookWars, enough to cover costs and pay off the NYU part of my student loans, which was a top priority. They wouldn't release my transcripts so I could apply for jobs, until I had paid off all their loans. Right-a real-life 'Catch 22'! Anyway, I can't think of many other sectors where that-the 'negative pickup'-is considered to be an acceptable business model.

"Now, I had done movies previously, I had done movies before BookWars. I went through the whole rigmarole with Charlie's Box, for instance, the indie drama I had produced and wrote and directed, made completely on film, back in 1991 after I graduated from NYU film school. So, I went through those steps again, contacting festivals, sending out materials, etc. Making contact with sales agents, trying to reach distributors. At that time there was no Withoutabox, or other online mechanized services where you can submit your video file or DVD to numerous festivals at once-DVDs even at that time were new. There was no Withoutabox, or Filmfreeway, or Reelport.com, all of these platforms where you could submit your video file and information once and have it automatically routed and propagated to different festivals. So it had to be done manually."

"And I did submit–as most filmmakers do–to Sundance. They had a midnight movie section which I thought would be suitable for the movie. Everyone who had seen BookWars up to that point felt that it would be a great match for their midnight movie section. And it seemed like we had a good shot at it, especially considering the New York producer, Michel, had screened at Sundance and had a special jury award for one of his movies previously. A movie called Jupiter's Wife. So I figured, okay, well here's a chance to get in at least at the midnight movie section. But, you know, as it turns out, it didn't get in. Not that it matters tremendously in terms of sales."

"Movies which screen at Sundance frequently have as a hard time finding real sales and distribution as non-Sundance movies, even with that seal of approval. But, even to this day, people I talk to in New York or San Francisco are mystified. They always say, 'Hey, why didn't [BookWars] get into Sundance? That was a great movie, a classic.'"

I admit I had wondered that myself.

"I think that has to do with politics, on some level. I

was not a known filmmaker; I was not established, was not from an elite circle, and I had few connections. Anyway, I think it really does make a difference if you're connected-it really does. And a lot of folks who break through early on, earlier than their unconnected peers, often do have that leg up. It's not a make or break thing though, of course-Jack Nicholson was famously unconnected. Jim Jarmusch did welding for a living, so I heard, before he broke through. Anyway, I wasn't really connected myself; as mentioned, my father had died when I was young, my mother was an immigrant from a working-class city in the UK [Liverpool] with a high school diploma. She went and earned her degrees later, hats off to her."

"In the end, the persistence and hard work, really bootstrapping your ass off will make up for the lack of connections to a significant degree. But there's a price, and I think I paid the price through a tremendous and persistent hit to my quality of life over the three or four years I was travelling around scraping up editing gear for that movie. Leaving a good startup job in San Francisco in the late 90's to go back to New York to complete the movie. I think that's something I would advise folks to watch out for if and when they bootstrap a project, startup, a business, what have you. The process can devour you. In retrospect, I have to say that was a real tossup decision to leave a steady job and domestic life on the West coast to go complete the movie. True, by that point I was possessed with an all absorbing focus to complete the project, do or die. But I mean, I haven't necessarily been raking it in or living large since the release of BookWars or Lost in New Mexico or Freedom Deal or other movie efforts. Then again, who knows what lies around the corner?"

"Anyway, I did submit it to several other notable fests, and it found its home for the premiere at the [New York] Underground Film Festival, which was still running at the time, that's where BookWars, had its premiere, at Anthology Film Archives. Back then, I didn't realize at that time the intricate connection between festivals, reviewers, and the whole circuit. For instance, the PR people, reviewers, festival programmers, they're all plugged into each other and remarking to each other, you know, [about] what is playing and what they can get a scoop on, either to show at their own festival or to do a writeup of the movie, and so forth."

"So when the very first review of BookWars came out in the NY Press, a New York Film Critics Circle review by

Matt Zoller Seitz, based on a preview screening at the New York Underground Film Festival...I was stunned. It was an overwhelmingly, tremendously positive review by a rigorous, seasoned reviewer. I didn't expect it, or any reaction at all, actually. As if I'd forgotten, by the time I completed it-since I was so spent and dazed-that it was actually meant ultimately to be seen by others, by an audience, and that they might connect with it."

"I remember, it was an afternoon-on West 4th Street actually-and I got the New York Press, looked at this review, the movie's very first review, and it was marvelous. It was mindblowing."

"And I wasn't seeking mindblowing reviews, although they're nice. I was seeking to finish the movie, because it had sort of exploded out of my life-exploded out of my psyche like an animal. And I needed to to...I don't want to use the word exorcise...but to fulfill it. So when I saw this review in the New York Press I had to lean against this fire hydrant. There's a big fire hydrant on the corner of LaGuardia and West 4th, and I leaned against it and read this review. My god, it's actually real. The movie is not just a dream, a phantom living in my head. And it continued to get some great reviews through various newspaper channels; through that festival, and through other festivals."

"And now that I'm thinking about it, I remember there was an accumulation of other strong reviews before the questionable review by Elvis Mitchell at The New York Times. Yes, that lifted my spirits and so forth. But I also wanted to sell it. I wanted to sell it, and I needed to sell it. I started thinking about, well, how to get this thing out there? How to get it out there and broadcast and so forth. And Michel, gratefully–this was a welcome thing–he had a connection with ARTE/ZDF, the buyer in Germany, Doris Heppe. He set up a meeting with her, and based on the final cut, I managed to negotiate an agreement to get an advance based on the exclusive premiere status of the broadcast of BookWars in Europe on ARTE/ZDF. I got an advance, based on that, but I also needed to re-cut the movie from 79 minutes down to 56:30 for TV."

I comment that that European TV deal, the first sale for the movie, must have been the proverbial oasis in a desert.

"That was very welcome. Every part of it: financially, artistically, you name it. And it boosted my spirits to know that the work, the product, whatever you want to call it, had value and was appreciated. Besides that, though, there was not much overt activity to push the movie or move the movie, as far as I could discern domestically. So I think, looking back on it, that there was a little bit of hesitance about promoting BookWars to a wider audience in the States, versus Europe. I don't know why. And I don't know if that has to do with the politics at the time, or if the co-producers were just ultra-busy, or possibly there was some pressure from the book project, but there was some apparent restraint in that aspect. Obviously, after all the effort and struggle, I was seeking every way possible to push and sell the movie."

"Even so, we went ahead and showed it at the Independent Filmmaker Project. Well, I had submitted it there. I forget what it's called now...the IFP Market I believe it was called at the time. And there we met a distributor, since we showed a rough or fine cut of BookWars. It was a new distributor called Avatar Films, and they were interested. They were just starting out and sort of poking around at the IFP Market for what sort of content they wanted to start off with. They were looking for their first film."

I ask for details, as I'm very curious about how the film business actually functions.

"We made a deal with them and, out of good faith–I was not even obliged to–I offered to give Avatar 10 percent of the Arte deal. The Arte/ZDF deal was set up before Avatar had come along, but would be concluded just after they would come on board, so I offered a compromise to the standard sales agent percentage and basically gave them like $3000, something like that. As a show of good faith sort of thing. The understanding was, and our agreement specified, that they would be doing TV broadcasts. They would not be focusing on theatrical, but focusing on TV broadcasts. And that was fine by me because, you know, theatrical is very tough and BookWars is a very niche movie. It's a New York movie, gritty, low-fi, so.... Clerks did it, but that's like a one-off; you can't use Clerks as a template."

"So I figured, well, surely TV will be a good stable for BookWars. As it turns out, the distributor then at some point decided to start doing theatrical instead, and they hadn't made any TV sales at all yet. Luckily–and this is what I would advise to emerging filmmakers, and other relevant bootstrappers–I had researched a lot about contracts with distributers before we signed, and I inserted a performance clause into the distribution agreement. I wrote it out, actually, researched and wrote it out. I had a performance clause implanted into the contract, which said, well, if they, Avatar, didn't make a certain amount in TV sales by such a date, then I had the right to take back the TV rights and attempt to sell it myself unimpeded. That would later come into play."

"So, Avatar Films, our new distributor, started to focus on theatrical exhibition instead. They picked up a couple other titles, and I guess they decided to become theatrical for whatever reason. Along those lines, they then requested that we make a 16mm print of BookWars, which is all fine and well, but it's kind of expensive, and not really that sellable beyond educational–you know, 16mm projection is neither here nor there, basically old school educational. And, you know, this was one of the more significant bad financial calls, I guess, of the whole process."

"But nobody really knew what they were doing, between myself, the co-producer Michel, or Avatar Films at that time. We were all kind of guessing and feeling our way along."

"Thus, I would say to anyone listening, or reading this–with any project you may be putting together–unless you are heavily subsidized through some means, then you've got to watch your dollars and cents like a hawk. Five grand is peanuts for a big budget movie, but is a chunk for me, and was back then as well. Looking back, I would say it's good for the filmmaker and producer and distribution partners to be very discerning about where the money is going, to make sure that everything spent, everything put in, has some metric which results in real value for the project and for the pockets of those involved as much as possible. This could apply to other new and emerging fields which are as yet untried and untested, in terms of monetization."

"For example, if you're thinking of producing content for AR or VR (Augmented Reality or Virtual Reality), which is still uncharted in terms of monetization, you should be sure that, unless you are subsidized, you are going to be able to cover the costs for the VR or AR gear, the production overhead, whatnot."

"And everyone should have skin in the game, actual money or assets invested. Be healthily skeptical of encouragement from those who don't have actual, tangible money or resources invested in the project...their thoughts, as well-meaning as they may be, are less likely to be rooted in the necessity of recouping costs and making sales."

Advice to live by!

"So despite the lack of funding, the movie went on to play decently, had some decent broadcasts and some respectable domestic and international exposure-especially considering its budget, which was near-zero. It got some great reviews. You know, it did its limited theatrical thing. But still, the meat and potatoes of that movie would be, and was in fact, TV. International TV turned out to be its strongest suit."

"And thanks to the performance clause I had put in the contract, I was able to take back those rights and to ramp up the TV sales. I would have wished that Avatar Films did better with the movie-selling it to TV and so forth. I wanted everyone to make some money off it if they could. But Avatar was also busy scoping up more projects to sell and building up their business. However it may work out, they didn't sell any TV. So, the performance clause date line came along and I said, you know, I'd like to take the TV rights back. And there was no problem with that; no one argued or anything like that."

"I took the rights back, made a trailer, a one sheet PDF, and researched the names and contacts of the international and domestic buyers as best I could–and bam! I made a string of sales, you know, right off the bat. SVT in Sweden; sold it to them twice actually. NHK in Japan...Metrochannels in New York. A little PBS. Some early streaming services paid decently for it actually too, I was surprised. That was back in 2001 or so, around the time, but just before, the burst of that bubble."

"Now big sales agents like Films Transit in Canada, Jan Rofekamp, they're great if you can get them to handle your movie. They declined BookWars because, as Jan told me, essentially, niche movies are great but they require a lot of work to sell through the secondary tiers: cable, and satellite. I guess it's like picking the morsels off of the buffet table when you really want to scoop in a big slab of roast beef."

"Which is what he does. Film Transit, and sales agents like that, they handle big blue-chip projects. So, for a smaller niche movie like what I had, I...had to make the sales myself and I had to negotiate those contracts and sales windows, all the sales parameters. That was really the only alternative left. There was another sales agent in the UK, but her outfit was folding up at the time. So it was really up to individual filmmakers to sell their own movies. So that's what I did. I didn't have any training or experience–I guess there's the essential bootstrapping mentality again, at the essential core-but I just put two and two together. I did some research, poked around on the Internet for different documentary one-sheets, made a trailer, sent those out in a single email to a lot of different broadcasters."

"So that's what happened with BookWars. Overall, despite the lumps and bumps, I'm satisfied artistically and I made some money off of it and I think it's a unique movie. It's really the only movie made in New York during the whole Quality of Life campaign, as seen from the street point of view. I'll talk about my other projects in detail at some later date-Lost in New Mexico, Freedom Deal, and others, they all have their interesting behind the scenes moments as well."

"It was the spirit of the movie, I guess, and the sort of benign, bootstrapping madness that pushed it forward-as well as the assistance of a lot of folks along the way, of course. The Montoya brothers helping out as co-producers in San Francisco, taking a chance on me; Alan Fulford in New Mexico. The fortuitous meeting with Michel in New York just around the time I'd started shooting. All those things came together to make it happen. All of them came together equally: Alan Fulford in New Mexico, the Montoya brothers in San Francisco,

Dennis Muldrow in San Francisco, Michel Negroponte in New York, and all of the people...and myself, obviously. I mean, I put in so much effort. Maybe too much effort! Oh well."

Considering everything I've thus far heard, I comment that there's a lot more to the movie-making process than most folks may see. Was it worth it-in the end, given all the struggle and sacrifice? Was the making of the movie worth the years of effort and struggle and sacrifice?

"Would I do it again if I could see what it would entail? That's a tough one. Well, I'm glad I made it, but if I knew what would go into making it, saw all the challenges just lying there in one row or pile-I probably would not have had the fortitude to proceed. So, in that sense, there are times when a bootstrapper has to break things down to their essential steps and not look at the big picture, the mountain of work and challenges, head lest a psychological overload occurs. That may sound counterintuitive, since folks are often talking about seeking the 'big picture'. But, from my experience at least, if you're caught up in a very challenging and tough process or situation, it's useful to avoid looking at the big picture, just to break things down one step at a time. "

The filmmaker brings us back to the present, to discuss a few other realities of the digital world.

"Now, cutting forward to 2016, you know, BookWars is just one of thousands of older movie titles. There's a sea of content out there, movies, music, games, you name it. Maybe one day the movie will get another day in the sun, or whatnot, for its historic value, who knows. But there's so much product out there now, because filmmakers have access to inexpensive editing gear, and can make movies about their grandmother or whoever–and just crank it out in two weeks. So, it's obviously not necessary to travel around to far-flung places to access different editing platforms like I did in order to make a movie. You can edit now even on a smartphone! Basic editing that is, but still..."

"Unfortunately, the present day is also the era of intellectual property being misappropriated without permissions of the owner–I think, in large part because of the 'sharing culture' that has emerged over the past decade. Everyone thinks digital work–movies, music, other media–is free. And, as a corollary, it seems as though if you somehow object to this–even if you're the owner of the content and have bust your ass and spent a lot of money to make it–you're just being difficult."

"For example, just recently there was this sort of socialist organization called the Henry George Foundation–no, the Henry George School, in Chicago. I happened upon them. Just once in a while, I'll do a Google search and see if there are any screenings of Lost in New Mexico, BookWars, or any of the tunes I've been producing lately."

"Anyway, there was this organization, this school, and they were doing a screening of BookWars, just this past May 2015; they had advertised the screening on their website, invited the public and all that. I was interested, because I didn't recall having a distribution agreement for public performance, though they may have purchased a public performance screener. So I sent them a nice email. You can look on the blog, actually–on Camerado.com–and you'll see. It started off nicely enough. I sent a respectable, outgoing email saying, 'Hey, I heard you just screened our movie, I hope it went well. I'm just wondering, you know, what about the Public Performance situation?'"

"And the email I got back from the guy–this guy, their leader I guess, ' Chuck'–had essentially stated 'We don't need rights to show it. We have Fair Use.'"

"Now, I'm aware of Fair Use; I know the laws, because

I have to defend myself and the work, you know, in terms of screenings throughout the years. And this was not fair use–they'd advertised it openly and invited the public, so it was not just a face-to-face classroom environment. They'd been doing this for a while, apparently, since they had many other movies openly listed and advertised on their site as well. I'd been nice about it initially–I mean, it should not be even my legal burden to track the parties who are abusing the property, but even so my outreach was nice enough."

"Anyway, these folks apparently believe in the consignment of privately produced intellectual property to the public commons. Their founder, a fellow named Henry George, established their economic philosophy in the 1800s before IP was around, so in that sense, it's an antiquated philosophy which could reasonably use some updating. They have no clue about the nature of IP–that work, effort, and money goes into producing content, and so they think it must be a common good like broadcast airwaves, or land...a common [good] that should belong to the masses. Even so, their namesake Henry George himself had stated that individuals have a right to extract value from that which they have fairly created. Go ahead and look it up yourself."

"I pointed that out to these guys. I said, 'Look, I put thousands of dollars into the mix out of my own pocket, traveled around...I'm still paying the movie off. This is not a commons–this is my property.'"

I ask if the "school" ever paid out.

"They wriggled and twisted, this guy 'Chuck,' their leader. I finally stated that I would end up doing a fundraiser to make up the difference and raise the complete screening fee on their behalf. But, really, I don't have time for that now, maybe later. Basically, their leader, this guy Chuck, said, 'Some of us are busy making a living'–as if the process of making the movie they'd just ripped off was not ass-busting hard work. Then he says, 'The board does not want to approve any amount...we can only pay you such and such an amount,' which was less than a quarter of a standard screening fee. Finally, he added: 'This offer expires August 1$^{st.}$.' I was thinking: do they make the same conditions to their landlord when the rent is due? 'We can only pay you this amount...and this offer expires shortly.' Amazing!"

"If they had done outreach to me initially, I could have reduced the screening fee significantly. But why do outreach to the copyright holder when it's easier to rip off the property, to steal it? Why spend five minutes, in aggregate, undertaking outreach to the filmmaker-copyright holder, when, according to your economic philosophy, there is no such thing as private IP or copyright?"

"I declined to take their reduced fee. Even though I sorely need the money–I'm still paying off the movie, and now I'm helping out a very poor family in Cambodia which is sending their kids to school for the first time. The single mother of the kids, who I've known for years, plays a ghost in my more recent drama, Freedom Deal: Story of Lucky, by the way."

"Anyway, by accepting the reduced amount, which was only grudgingly offered with a deadline and caveats anyway, I would have validated the Henry George School's behavior and theft, and I would have thus supported the notion that digital property has no value–something I totally disagree with, and which would ultimately hurt my fellow filmmakers, writers, musicians, and other producers."

"Just because it's digital, intangible, doesn't mean it doesn't exist or have value. The broadcast spectrum is intangible, but it's been auctioned off for millions of dollars. I mean, you go to a restaurant and order a steak that's $25-after you've eaten the steak, you have to pay for it. You can't run out on the bill, that's not proper or lawful by any reasonable standard. And you can't grudgingly offer to pay the restaurant only $5 after you've been busted trying to run out the door either."

"So, I think the incident with this strange school is just a symptom of the times-the contemporary sharing, or 'commons' culture we're in now-well, they call it sharing. It's basically just theft unless the copyright holder consciously donates their property, transfers it to the commons permanently. That happens, and that's nice, why not? But it's not obligatory...no copyright holder or producer is obliged to consign their work to the commons just because that's the trend. Producers who have an investment in their work tend to disagree with any forcible abrogation of their rights and property."

"The challenge of the era for many creatives, including bootstrapping creatives-at least those working in any kind of digital medium. The Internet economy and shared culture has degraded the value of digital goods, or goods that can be digitized if they were not produced digitally, to a point that many people can no longer perceive or comprehend that actual effort and money has gone into the production of the work. It's so freely and readily available–it must not have any costs attached to it. And that's just not true.

"If nothing else, I hope the bootstrapping behind the making of this movie could stand as a testament to the actual effort, time, and money that can go into the production of a digital work."

APPENDIX 1: RECOMMENDATIONS TO EMERGING CREATIVES

Editor's Note: the filmmaker has offered these recommendations to folks of all stripes-creatives, entrepreneurs, or otherwise

*Watch your cash flow and costs. Do not quit a job or borrow money to complete a creative project that has a significant degree of speculation involved in its sale, recoupment or distribution-no matter how passionate, or obsessed you may be with the undertaking (*unless you are subsidized and can sustain the risk and possible loss). If you are not subsidized, be mindful of folks, well-meaning as they may be, who may encourage you to throw caution to the wind and "go for it," i.e., to fund a project on credit cards or loans. Do they have any skin in the game? Do they have any real effort, money or time at stake or invested in the project? Are they subsidized, through grants or other assets, and therefore (wittingly or not) detached from some perspectives regarding practical livelihood issues? This is your life and your project, to complete or not complete, as you see fit. And you are accountable in the end if it is your project.

*Do not take out any student loans to fund an education. If you can't afford it without borrowing, then scale down or find a less expensive alternative. This goes for film, the arts, humanities, law, sciences, what have you. Do whatever it takes to stay out of the debt-trap.

*Do not compare your progress or metrics with others in your field without maintaining some healthy, balancing skepticism. Everybody has a different arc, different rates of maturation, and different levels of subsidy. That "career-comet" who lands a string of big editing gigs straight out of school may have an uncle who owns a postproduction studio. The scrappy, 'struggling indie director' may actually have folks with a townhouse (and couch) in Brooklyn. The acclaimed filmmaker may come from an established family with significant connections and subsidizing assets. As Voltaire says, "Hoe your own garden"–mind your own path and try to make sure that everything you do is its own reward.

*Storytelling will always be with us, but the technology behind the storytelling is constantly changing. As can be seen in this book, major shifts in postproduction technology–from linear to non-linear editing–were disruptive and presented new variables in the making of BookWars. The resulting process changed the budget, the costs, and the course of the project–the course of my life. My advice would be to pay attention to every side of the changing technologies in your field, whatever your field may be. And the changes may be a double-edged sword. That is to say: processes may be made easier or more efficient with the new technology, but may also result in a systemic change in the topography of your field, for better or for worse. In the independent movie world, cheap and accessible non-linear desktop editing made it easier than ever to put together a feature movie. Gone were the days of hunting down affordable non-linear editing suites, such as I had done during the editing of BookWars. One result of this new accessibility, however, was a glut of content. This in turn challenged curators' and programmers' capacities to manage, curate, and purchase titles. And what about the Internet? Will it completely decimate the world of film just as it did the world of music?

*Don't work too much on spec. [Speculation] You may have to work on spec initially, but after you've invested in putting together a portfolio or projects that you're satisfied with, folks (producers/hiring managers/etc.) should have a strong enough sense of your capability such that you can stop working on spec at that point if you choose to.

*Don't spend money from an apparently concluded deal until the actual numbers are in the bank in some verifiable, liquid form. For example: I made a deal for BookWars with a notable domestic independent film broadcaster. After much negotiation, in writing (by email) we settled on a sum. I was told, in writing, "It's a deal-let's paper it." And in the meantime, I was instructed to send the master tape, which I did, and it wasn't sent back for any technical reason and it was confirmed to be acceptable. I signed the W9 for tax purposes, sent that to them. Again, they confirmed the deal was concluded; they were just drafting the documents. And, according to all the other deals I'd done with SVT, Arte/ZDF, NHK, Metrochannels and others, this deal was moving in the same way and was just as solid.

I checked again to make sure everything was solid. "We're just drafting the paperwork" I was told. I had their confirmation in writing and they had accepted my master tape and the tax forms. This is considered, legally, to be substantial. So I invested some money, about half my liquid capital at the time, on the development of a new movie called Final Countdown, which was intended to be a follow-up to my second completed feature, Lost in New Mexico. Again, all statements and signatures on tax documents and in other areas supported the fact that this was a concluded deal.

Only after I had gone ahead and invested into my next feature, did I get an emailed note from that buyer that they "would have to withdraw from the deal." I was irritated, especially since that buyer stated it seemed that I was being too "hesitant," which was clearly not the case. And besides that, I'd just spent half of my limited capital on a new project, which now meant that my livelihood and finances were suddenly negatively impacted beyond a reasonable level.

They were grasping at straws to get out of the deal, and I guess something had gone wrong from their end. Even so, they had to honor their side of the deal or provide a kill-fee if they sought any normal exit. I noted that I had sent the master and the tax documents promptly, and all other materials right away. And finally, I explained that I invested money into my next movie based on the deal, based on their written word, and that our deal had already been formalized, according to several legal advisors and common protocol.

I asked for an industry standard kill-fee of 10%. The buyer at this film channel refused to work with the situation or to assume any accountability for their buyer who had formalized the agreement. They stated in the end that I should "talk to their legal department." So there you go, via an in-depth mini-case study: in this sector or industry at least, I'd suggest only spending the money from a concluded deal when the actual numbers appear in your bank account, despite the track record or reputation of the buyer or partner.

*As a corollary to the above: if and when you are screwed over, the symmetry of the situation has a great bearing on the final outcome. If you are not a name, you will be portrayed as the culpable party if the incident is serious enough. (But then again, the deal would likely not be pulled if you are an established name.) You are expected to take it, not to push back or try to defend your position. If you do push back, even if you are in the right, you may well be portrayed as the "bag guy" or "bad girl." Due to the fact that it is an asymmetrical relationship, the other, larger offending party will be able to mobilize more resources to cast doubt upon the incident and your role in it.

I'd say the only exception to the usual ways this sort of asymmetrical situation could play out would be an instance where the larger entity voluntarily and spontaneously agrees to some remedy without resort to any formal means. Beyond this, a limited number of nontraditional methods have in the past been utilized to create leverage against a larger offending party; we can see the latter sort of behavior manifested in the hacking* of the Sony Pictures website in the lead up to the release of The Interview (*kindly note that I don't support or agree with those actions).

*Keep an eye out for other similar but nonaffiliated projects which may be underway. Their key stakeholders may view your project (and yourself) as an existential threat, and they could try to torpedo your hard work. As mentioned, this occurred during the final stages of the production of BookWars, with regards to the street bookseller book project mentioned earlier. Learn about politics. Be bland and affable as possible, even if you're exhausted, and especially if you're not a 'name'.

Later, you may be able to speak your mind more openly when you're established in your field.

*As mentioned, it's useful to be as bland and affable as possible, especially if you're working in a small or insular sector. I don't know what the solution is if your personality is naturally a bit edgy. Take an etiquette course? Not sure. I have regrettably offended folks in the film/documentary sector without meaning to, due to this factor. Social landmines can be numerous in any small, tight-knit insular environment (art world/film/music/academia/etc.), and if your feelers aren't out at all times you may unwittingly precipitate a mobbing attack with yourself and your project as the targets. This is especially true if you are a newcomer to the environment. Personally, I find it very challenging to be bland and affable all the time, while simultaneously trying to execute a sustained project while under financial stress.

Along those lines, one corollary could be: consider carefully before embarking upon any project which will induce a level of sustained stress, including financial stress, such that your personality and outlook may change. It's not worth it. In my case, the production of BookWars involved such significant long-term stressors that I couldn't fully appreciate or savor the work when it was finally completed–numbed and dazed as I was. And I was made edgier, and less bland and affable as a result, I think.

Another corollary could be: make sure you have a producer or team member who can be the "bad cop" if need be to repel intruders, if and when someone comes along to screw with your project. This will likely happen at some point, by the way. I've experienced this phenomenon with several other projects besides BookWars, in different fields. In any case, it may not be appropriate for you, as director/creator/manager, to undertake the role of the bad cop/"tough" producer, since you will become a lightning rod for further interference. Besides, you will need to focus on the creative and managerial tasks at hand. If you are a filmmaker, ideally you would have both a "tough" producer (or key team member) as well as a "nice" producer (or key team member), in the event interference crops up that needs handling.

*It's OK to take a break; it's OK to do something else besides your stated passion for a while. And you may change to a new passion. After all this focus on making movies for the past quarter century, I've started working in music again, and have put movie making on the back burner for a while. I've found music to be more Dionysian than filmmaking, which is in my view the most Apollonian of the plastic arts. Let me fill you in: a while back, after completing my second feature movie, Lost in New Mexico, I'd gone to Greece to visit a girlfriend at the time, while trying to reassemble myself after that effort. That was also a tough, ass-kicking, no-budget project by the way–but that's another story. I went to the temple of Apollo in Delphi, where the old oracle used to hang out and deliver her prophecies, so I could sniff the air for some wayward thoughts that might be useful. And, wandering in the groves below the temple, I had that realization. Herman Hesse expresses the same notion in his book Steppenwolf–that our supposedly fixed and rigid personalities or self-concepts are actually numerously, infinitely multi-faceted. You may find that you have a similar, insight to do something else for a while-or as a new life path. Roll with it!

You contain multitudes. I remain skeptical of those who state, sometimes dramatically (for effect?) that they "will die if they can't make movies" (*or write books, or act, etc.). That is, if they can't practice their single and only stated craft. I have heard some say they are "terrified if they have no film project happening." This all was standard ideological fare at film school during the early 90's. The fact is, you will die without water, without food, without air, without shelter. But you will not die if you can't make a movie. Or run any particular business. Or if your line of clothing doesn't work out, or if your tech startup doesn't work out. Or if your restaurant doesn't work out, what have you. Just relax. My respected teacher, the late Israeli filmmaker and lecturer Milek Knebel, used to say along these lines: "Think of it all as a shirt you can take off and put on or change at will."

APPENDIX 2: PHOTOS & MEDIA

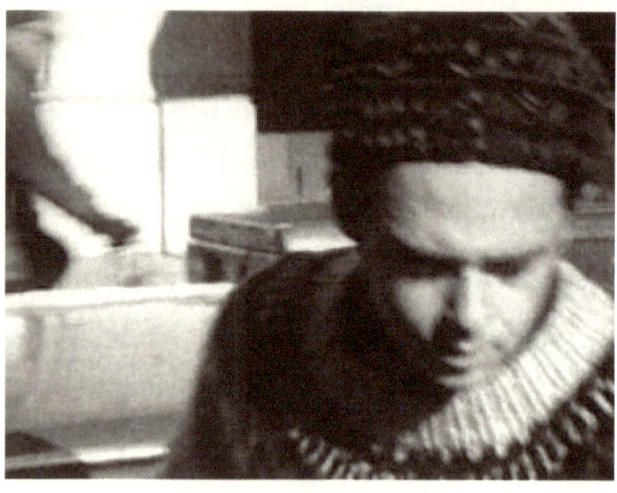

Bootstrapping filmmaker Jason Rosette at his book table on W4th & Mercer streets, NYC.

Still frame from 'BookWars' (2000)

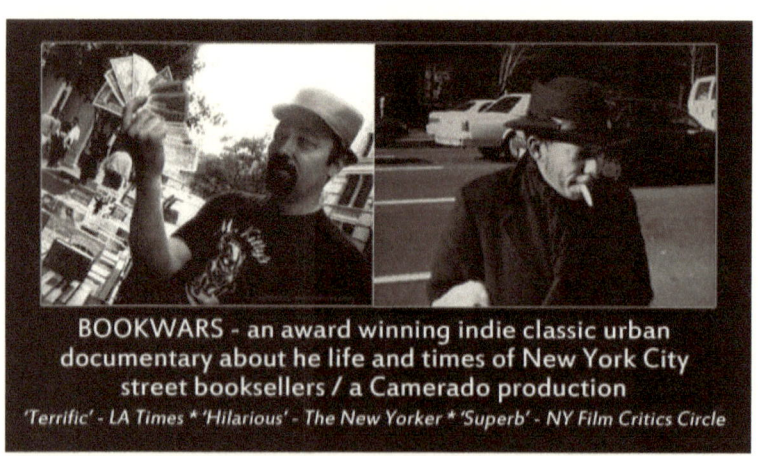

Video on Demand (VOD) banner for the project, multi-purposed from existing graphic content.

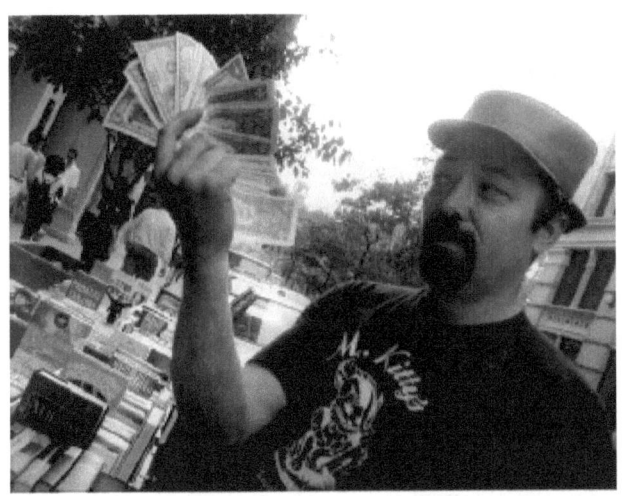

Street bookseller, artist and bootstrap entrepreneur Peter Whitney holds aloft a wad of cash earned at the bookstand; economic self-sufficiency is key for many sidewalk booksellers. (Photo: J Rosette)

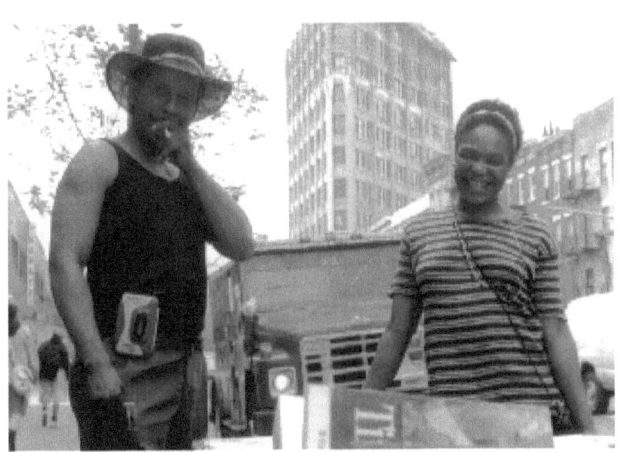

Sidewalk bookseller, Marvin, and his gal at his bookstand on 6th Avenue (Photo: J Rosette)

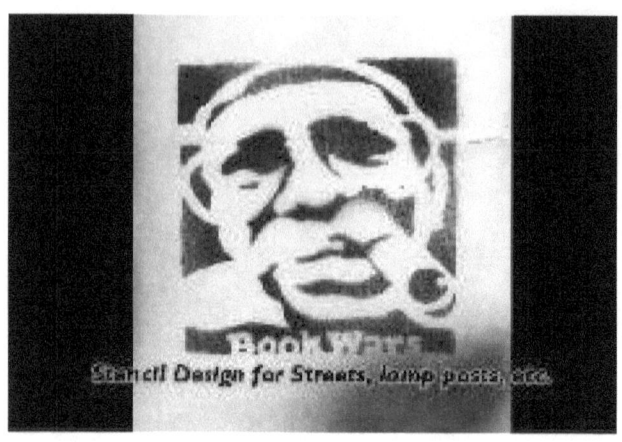

Bootstrap guerilla marketing for BookWars, using spray painted stencils around New York. The best time to go out was around 4 or 5 AM, in the gap between night life and daytime.

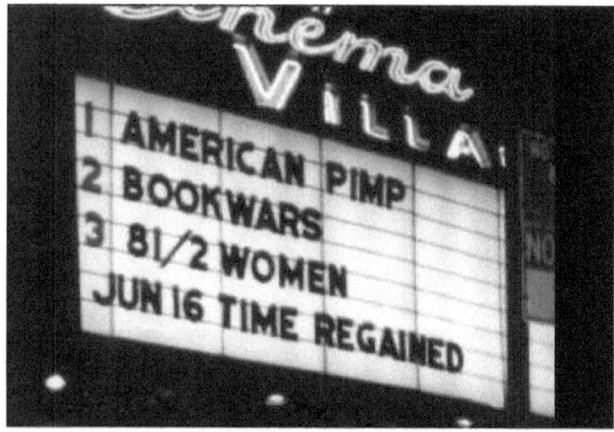

A hard-earned New York City theatrical release, after years of bootstrapping the movie forward.

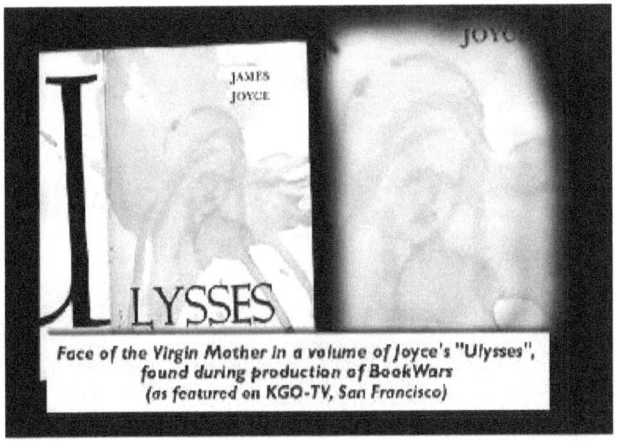

Face of the Virgin Mother in a volume of Joyce's "Ulysses", found during production of BookWars (as featured on KGO-TV, San Francisco)

More Bootstrap Marketing: A volume of Ulysses with a Virgin Mary shaped coffee stain was 'discovered' by filmmaker Jason Rosette while editing the movie in San Francisco. Local TV station KGO-TV aired a segment about it, granting BookWars valuable free airtime which boosted the project's exposure.

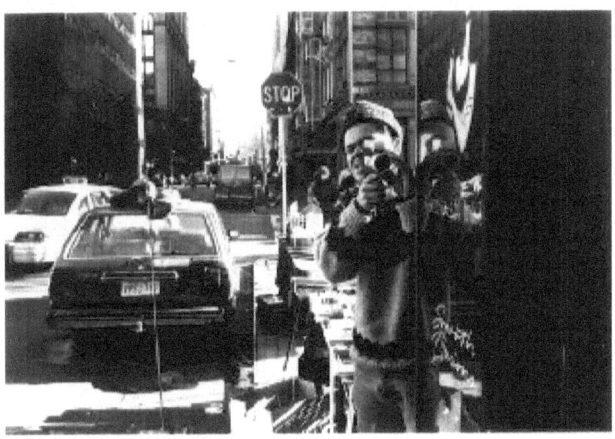

Bootstrapping filmmaker Jason Rosette shoots on film at the corner of W4th and Mercer streets in New York City. A wide range of cameras were used, depending on availability.

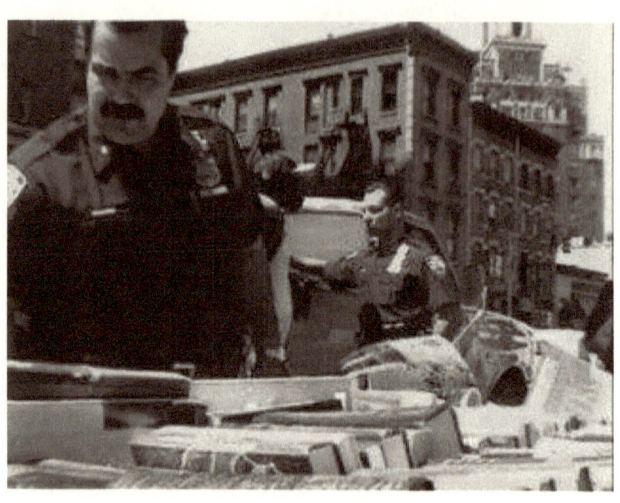

The NYPD force Slim to break down his table of books on 6th avenue; the cited reason was 'lack of a tax ID card' (From BookWars)

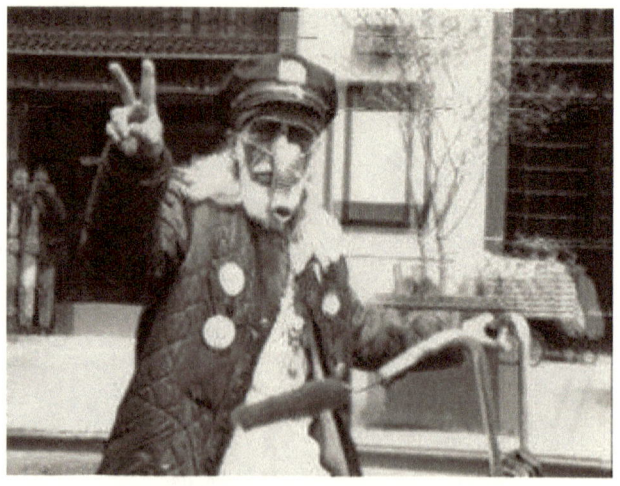

Rich characters of the public forum contribute to the life of the city; without a living public forum, the quality of life will be diminished. (From BookWars)

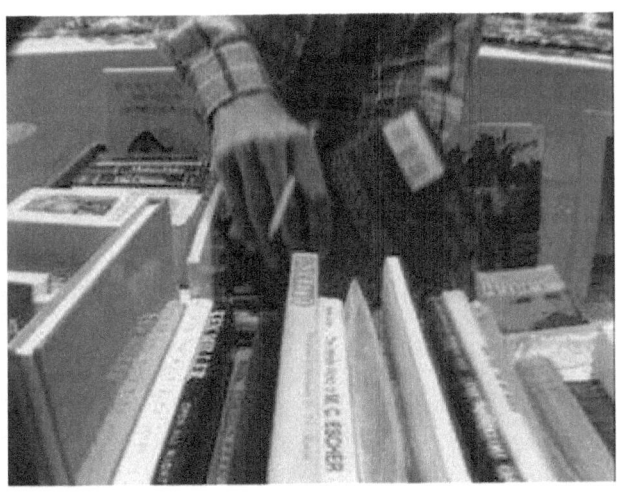

Literature and hardbound books tended to sell better on W4th street...

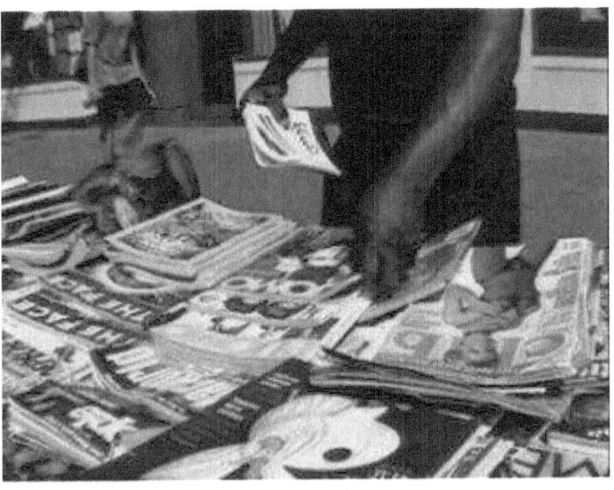

...while fashion, soft porn, and art magazines found a home on 6th avenue. The busier pedestrian corridor on 6th avenue resulted in a different business model. (From BookWars)

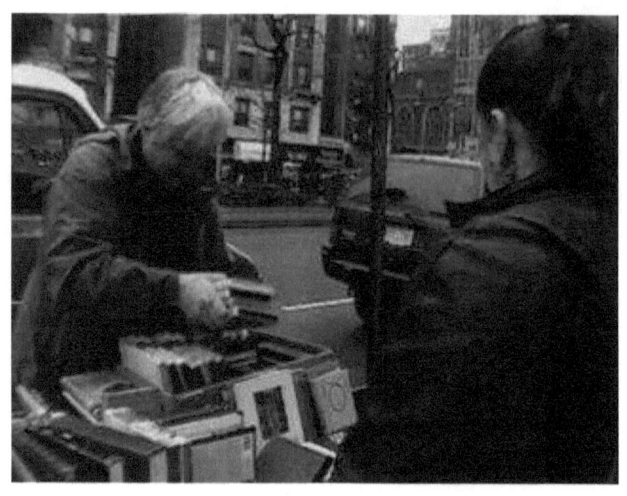

Margueritte, at her book stand on the Upper West side; women were the minority amongst street vendors in New York City. (From BookWars)

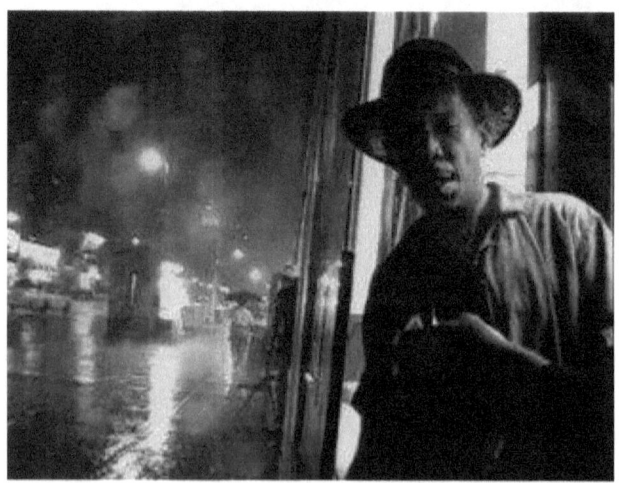

Booksellers Marv and Ron (in doorway), braving the rain on 6th avenue. (From BookWars)

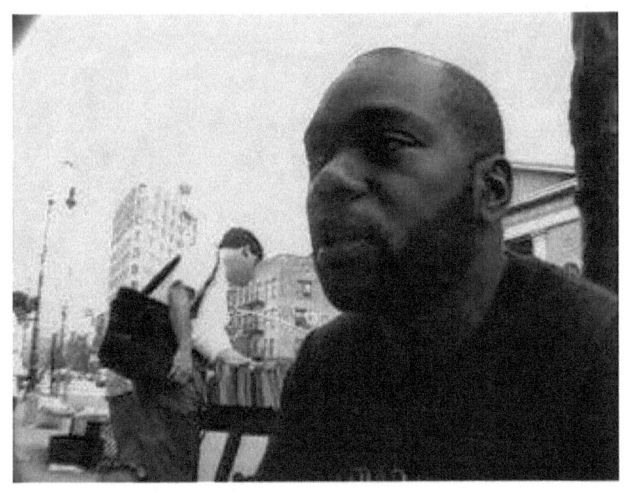

Sidewalk bookseller Ron Harris near his table on 6th avenue. (From BookWars)

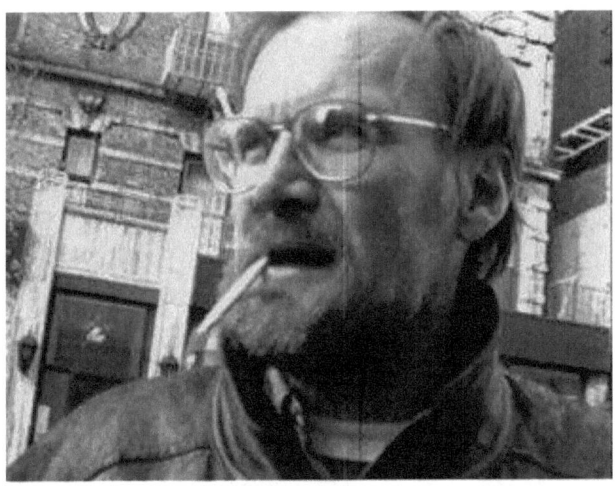

Polish Joe had no regular selling spot, and would set up in different parts of downtown Manhattan. (From BookWars)

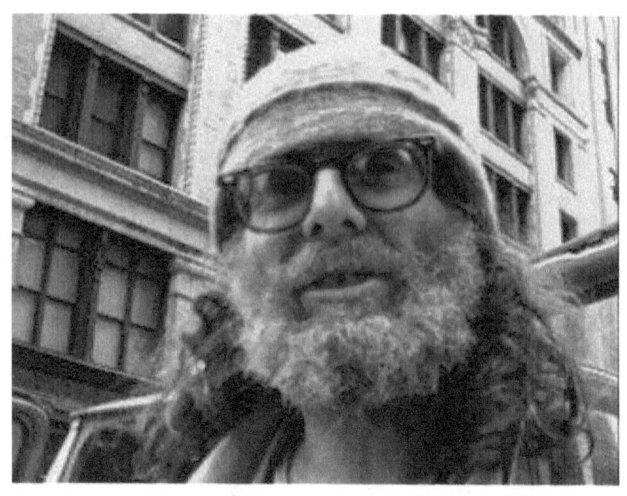

Sidewalk bookseller Everett Shapiro on West 4th street is prepared for the cold; even so, Everett wore shorts all year round. (From BookWars)

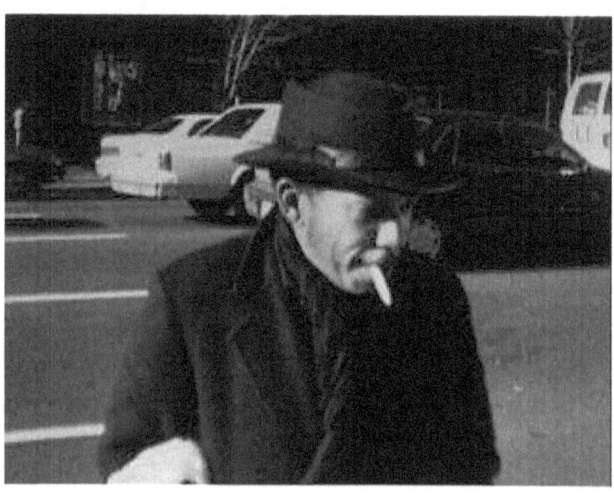

Winter on 6th avenue; Marv wears his trademark black hat (From BookWars)

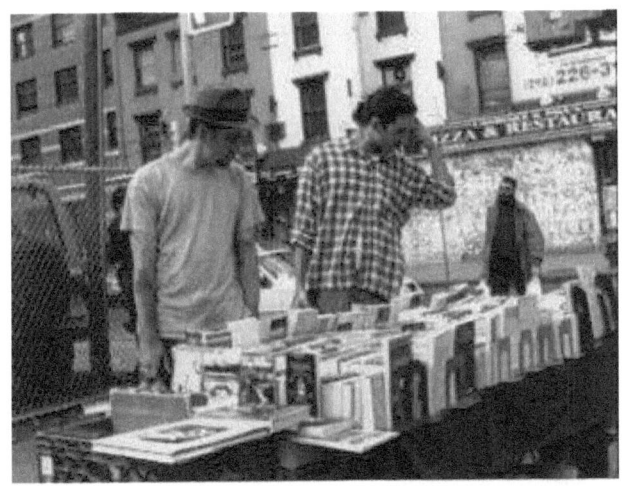

The bootstrapping filmmaker's table set up on 3rd avenue and 12th street. As books were sold, more tape and film was purchased, and shooting could continue. (From BookWars)

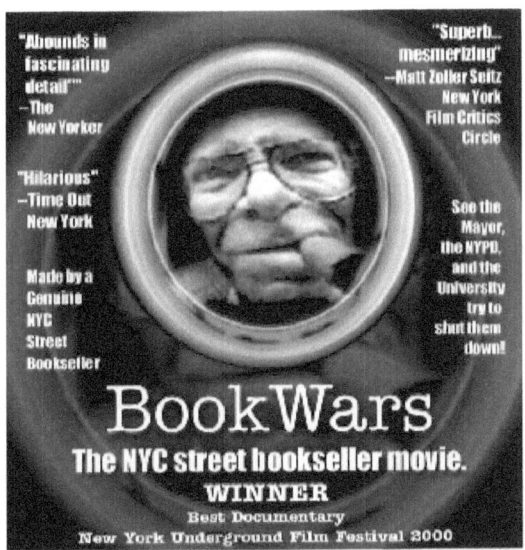

Theatrical ad for BookWars, as it appeared in various weeklies in New York City upon its release. The filmmaker bootstrapped all marketing, press releases, and PR to conserve cash.

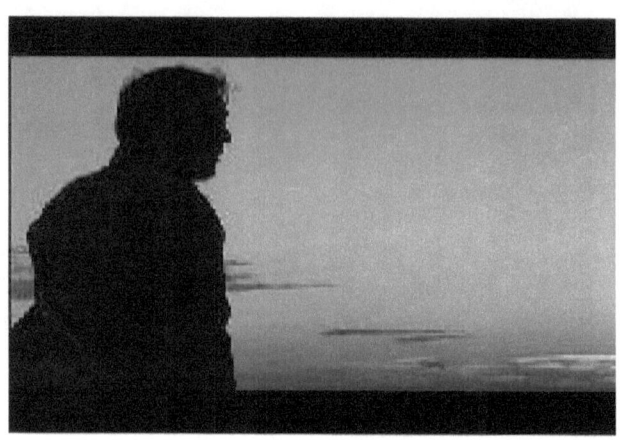

Screenshot from the filmmaker's 2nd feature, the multicultural road movie, 'Lost in New Mexico'. Bootstrapped on a low budget, the movie is available on Google Play, iTunes, Amazon, and other platforms. ('Great road pic'- Angelika Entertainment, NYC)

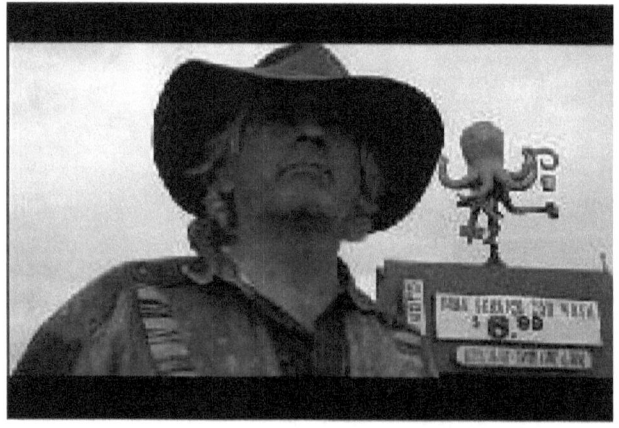

The mysterious Dr. Kurt Morell, played by Dr. Alan Rice

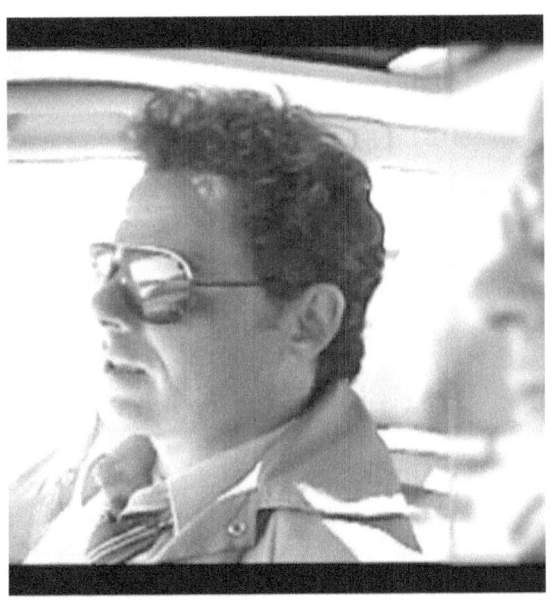

The bootstrapping filmmaker, Jason Rosette appearing as Federal Agent Carl Wisconsin. A member of SAG [Screen Actors Guild] the filmmaker put his membership on hiatus in order to appear in his own movie without breaking union rules.

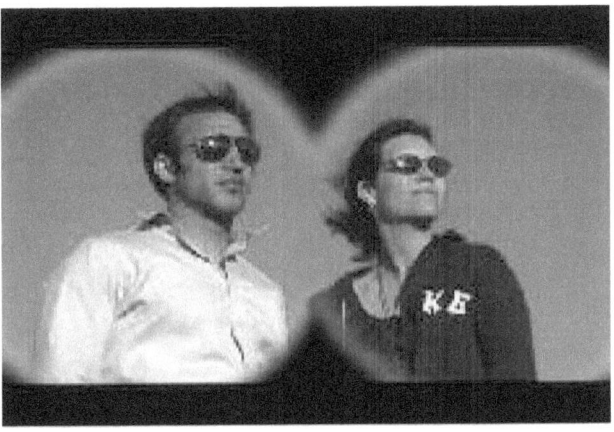

Jaime Estrada, left, as undocumented immigrant Javier Apollinaire; Drea Pressley, right, as the young fugitive, Susan

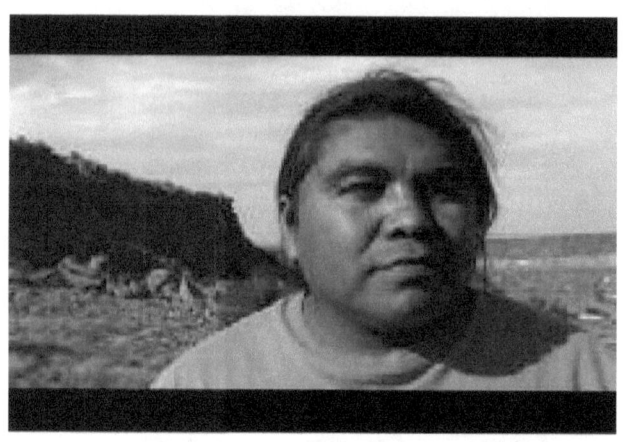

Native American actor David Paytiamo, as 'Lonnie'

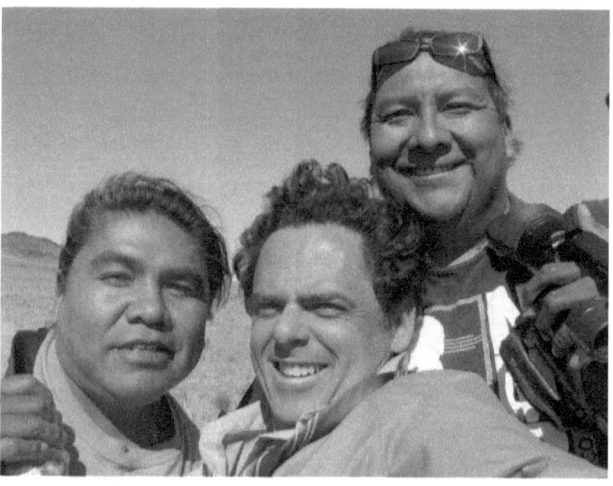

David Paytiamo and 2nd unit cameraman Dale Waseta, with the filmmaker shooting pickup shots for 'Lost in New Mexico'.

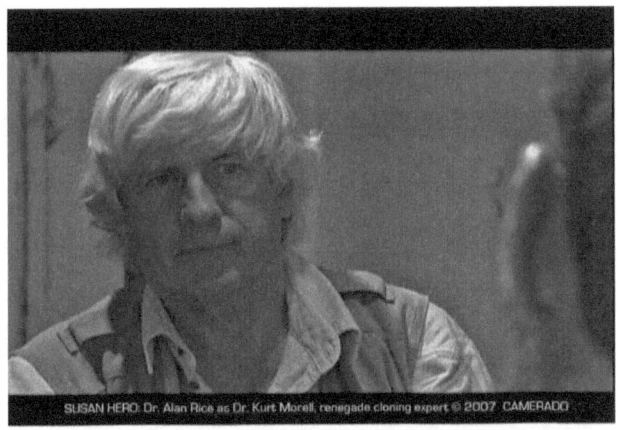

Dr. Kurt Morell (Alan Rice) holds Javier Apollinaire hostage in 'Lost in New Mexico'. Bootstrapping occurred frequently throughout the shoot: this scene was lit with high intensity bulbs from Walmart, which were then carefully re-boxed and returned.

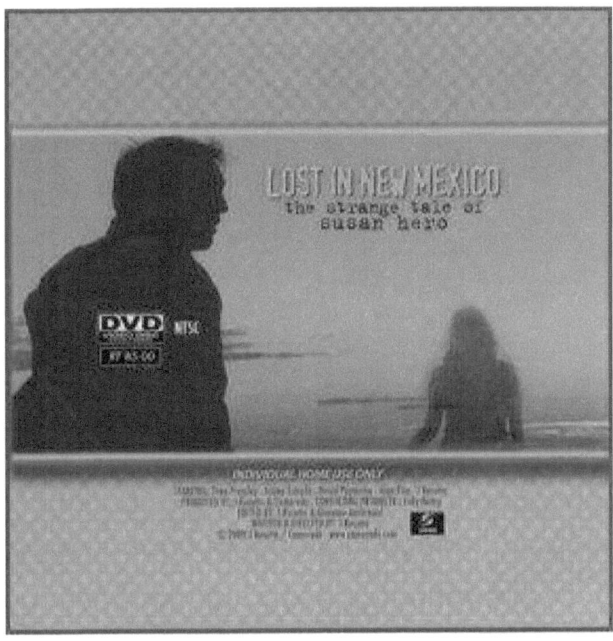

DVD package art from 'Lost in New Mexico'

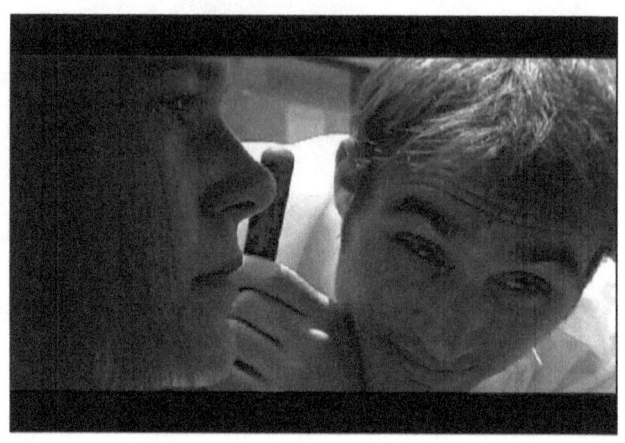

Javier Apollinaire encounters the young fugitive, Susan Hendricks–little does he know, he will soon be joining her.

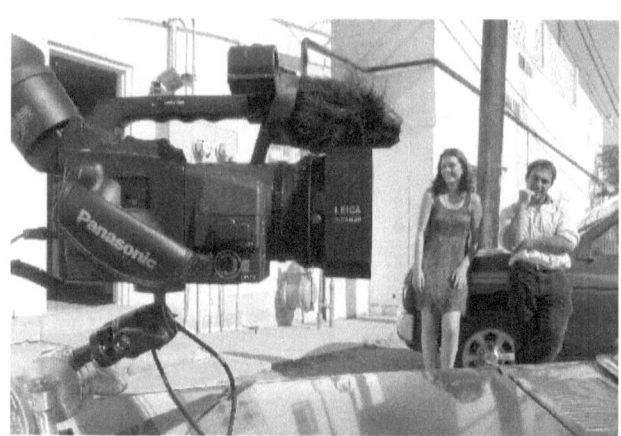

Shooting 'Lost in New Mexico' with a light car rig, while talent wait in background. All gear, including rigs, camera, sound and more would be sold off to pay for post-production.

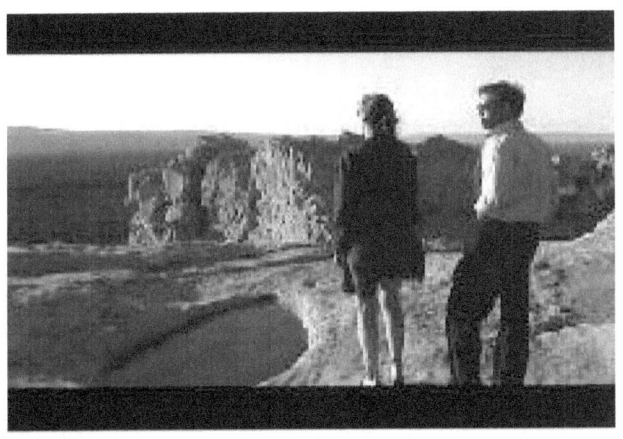

The incredible landscapes of El Malpais ('The Badlands') add production value to a scene in the bootstrapped feature road movie, 'Lost in New Mexico'.

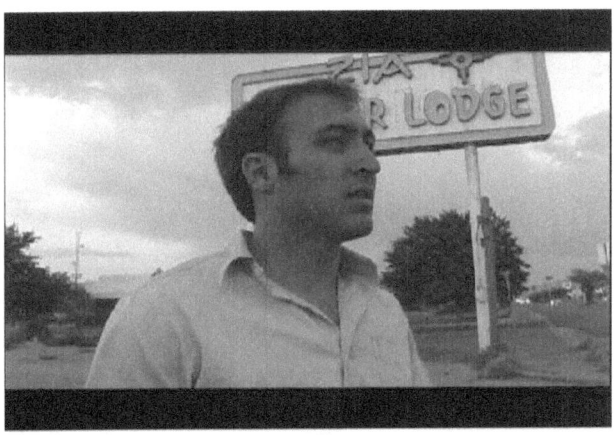

Illegal immigrant Javier Apollinaire (Jaime Estrada) decides what to do, and where to run, in a key moment in 'Lost in New Mexico'.

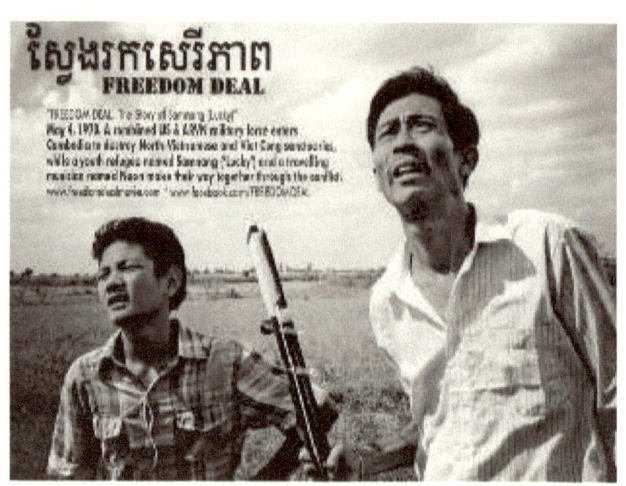

Protagonists from the supernatural Asian historical dramatic project, Freedom Deal: Story of Lucky. Shot on location in Cambodia, bootstrapping filmmaker Jason Rosette directed the movie in Khmer language.

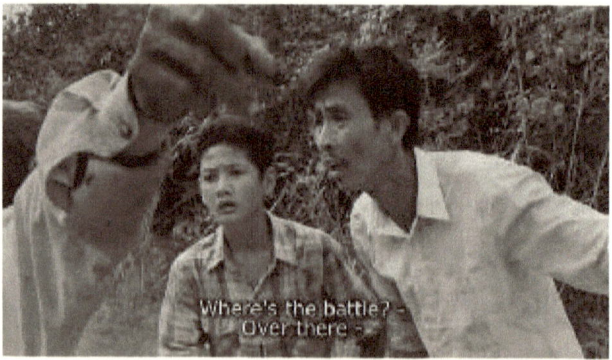

Darith Khoun (left, playing 'Lucky'), and Sok Polynn (right, playing the traveling wedding musician), find their way through the brewing conflict in 'Freedom Deal: Story of Lucky'

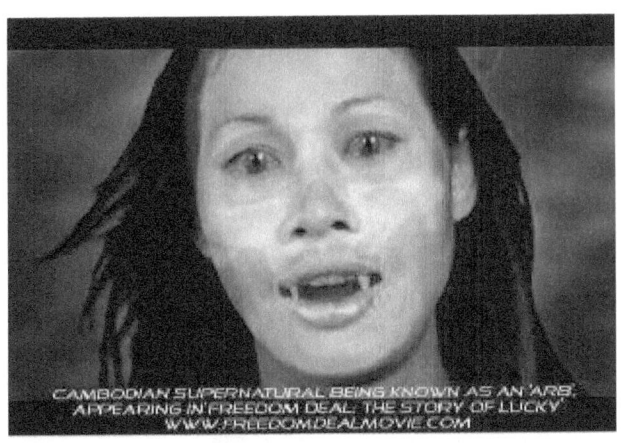

Supernatural being known as an 'Arb', appearing in 'Freedom Deal: Story of Lucky'. Written, directed and edited by Jason Rosette- as 'Jack RO'- the story is set along the Cambodia-Vietnam border during the US-ARVN incursion into Cambodia in 1970.

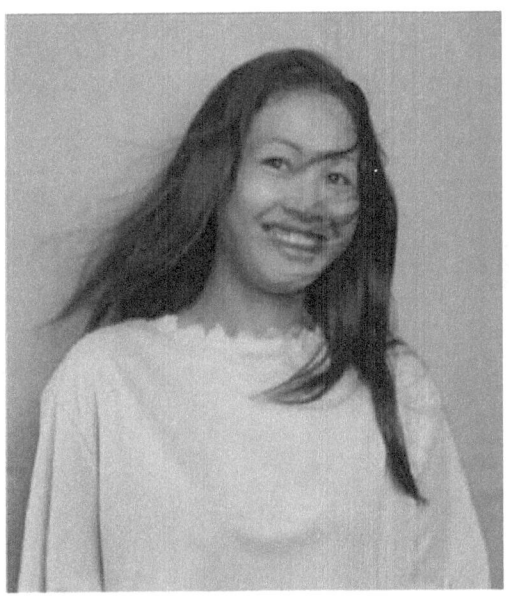

DIY green screen in Phnom Penh, Cambodia, during the shooting of the supernatural 'Arb' material. Seen here is Ms. Ran Lun

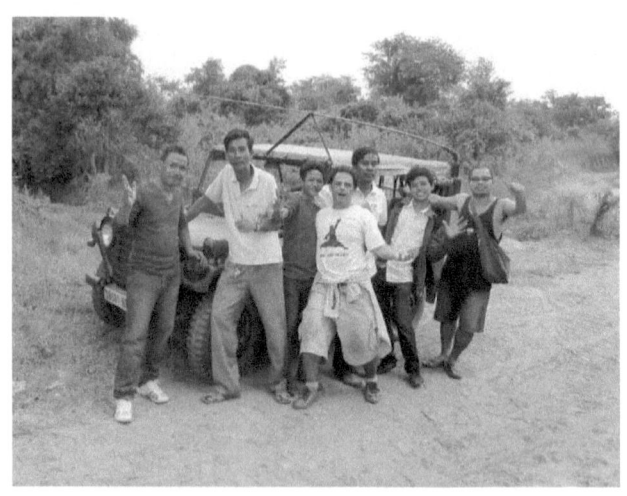

Partial team with period vehicle, a Vietnam War era Jeep, in Kandal province, Cambodia. Writer-Director Jason Rosette (as Jack RO), seen at center.

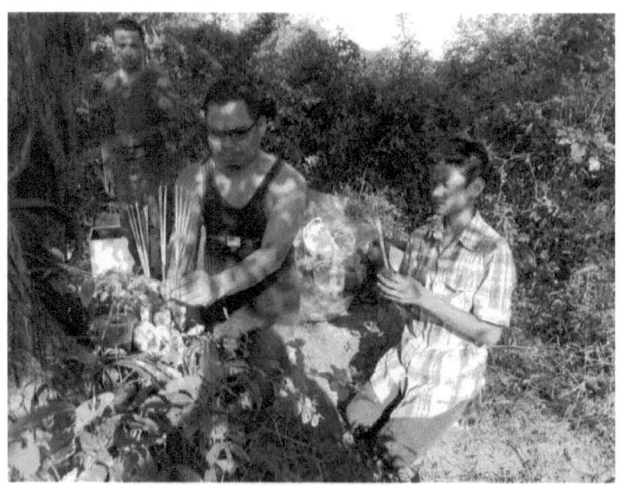

Offering prayers before shooting 'Freedom Deal' in Cambodia.

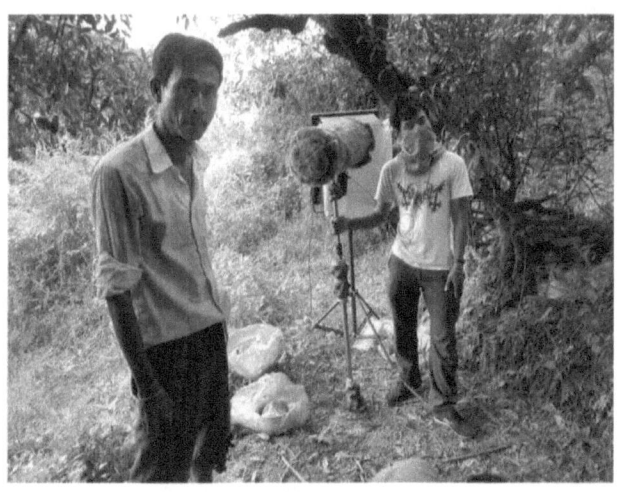

Bootstrapping it...yet again. Sound recordist Tieng Ratha with a homemade zeppelin on an extendable mop handle, using to cut wind noise during the shoot of 'Freedom Deal: Story of Lucky'. The zeppelin was made from a fake fur jacket stitched to a chicken wire frame.

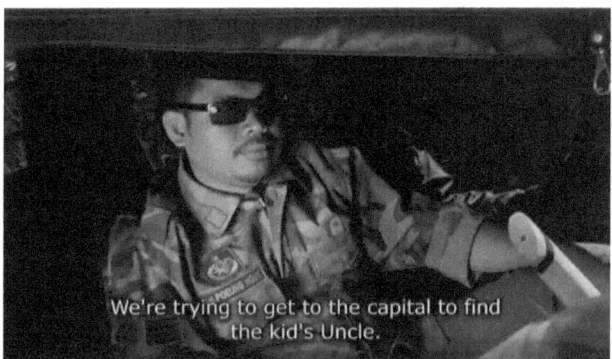

Socheat Sok as the Lon Nol military commander in 'Freedom Deal: Story of Lucky'. Socheat was slated to appear only as the driver of the Jeep, but he proved so effective at learning the lines during rehearsals, that he was swapped in for this role instead.

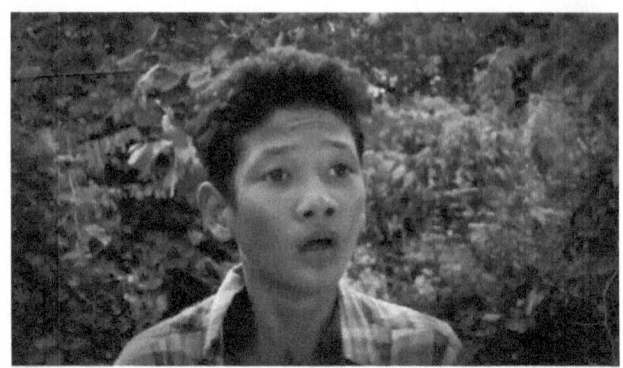

First time actor Khoun Darith ('Lucky') calls for help in 'Freedom Deal' Darith, a student at the Royal University of Fine Arts in Cambodia, nonetheless gave a very convincing performance.

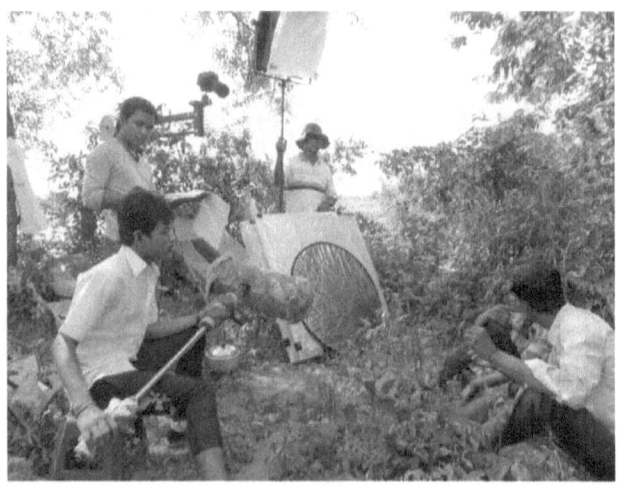

Bootstrapping it in Cambodia–all crew members were trained for the production.

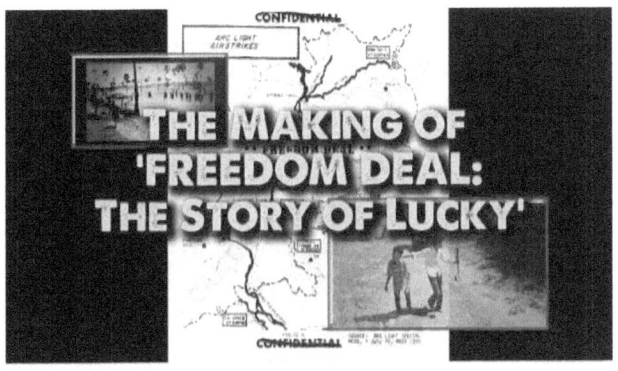

The making of 'Freedom Deal: Story of Lucky' is a story in itself; See a behind the scenes 'making of' video on Youtube

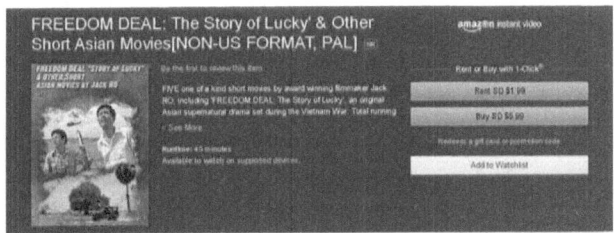

See 'Freedom Deal: Story of Lucky' on Amazon, along with other short movies by bootstrapping filmmaker Jason Rosette

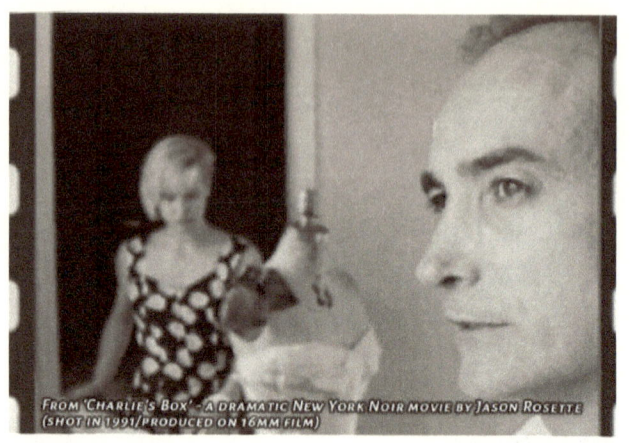

Band-aid Frank (Ralph Feliciello) and No Name Nancy (Victoria Kelly) in bootstrapping filmmaker Jason Rosette's first independent drama, 'Charlie's Box'. The movie was shot on 16mm film in 1991 shortly after graduating from NYU Film School.

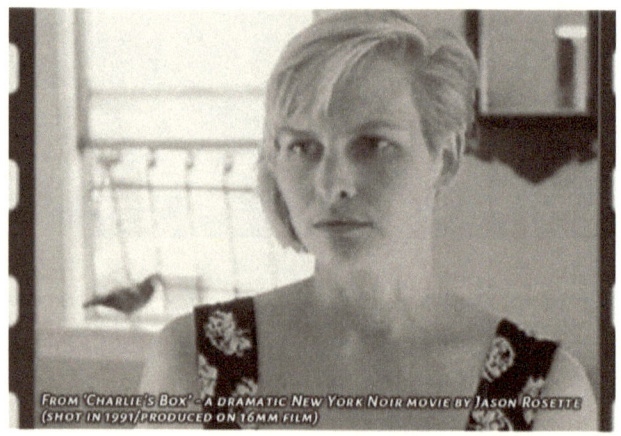

No-Name Nancy discovers a stranger–Band Aid Frank–has entered her apartment. The pigeon on the windowsill was trained by the filmmaker to be tame, over the course of several weeks.

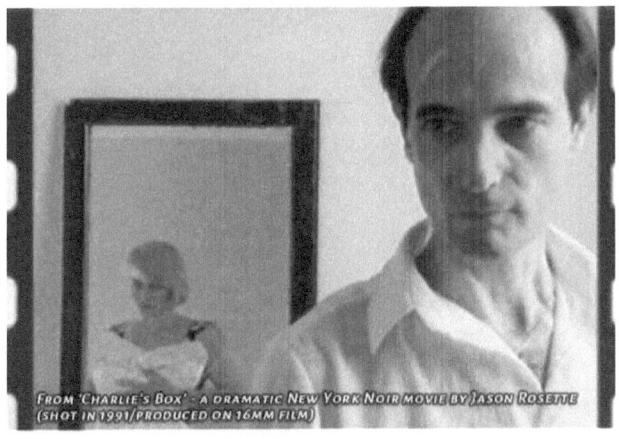

Band-Aid Frank admires Nancy's handiwork...but something else is on his mind!

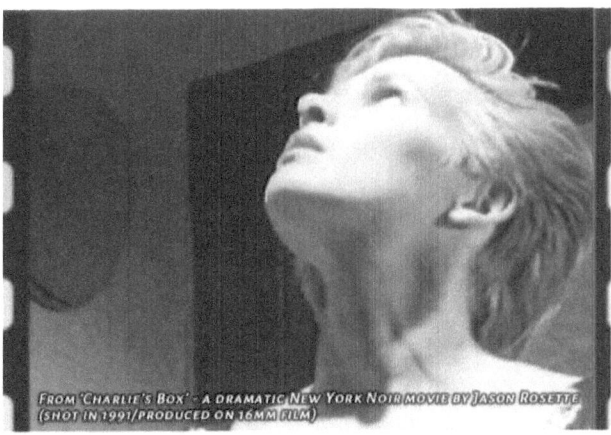

Nancy follows Frank up to the roof- something's going on up there.

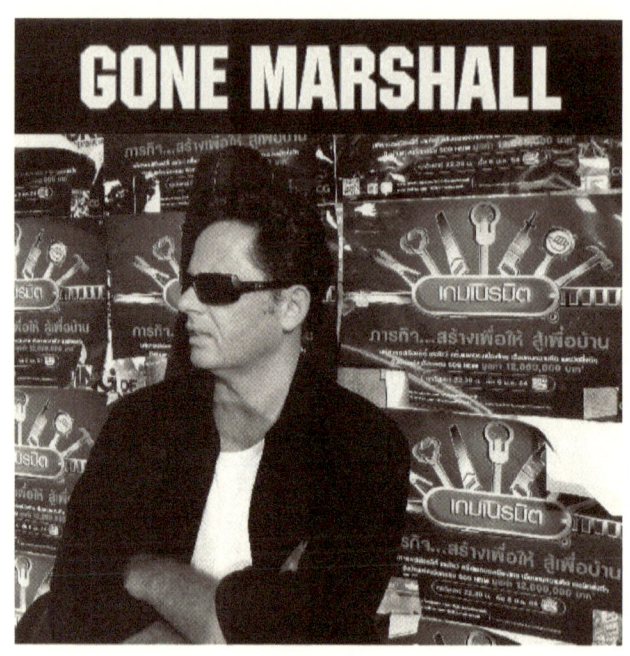

From film to music: the bootstrapping filmmaker as alt rocker, Gone Marshall

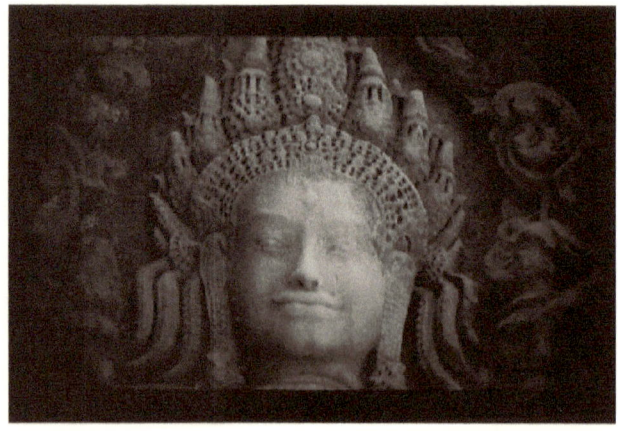

An Angkorian carving, located near the bootstrapping filmmaker's current location in Siem Reap, Cambodia.

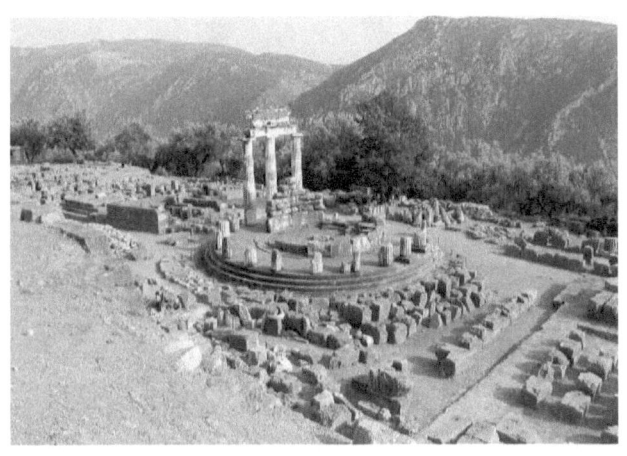

The temple of Apollo in Delphus, Greece, site of the ancient oracle. By Arian Zwegers (Delphi, Tholos Uploaded by russavia

[CC BY 2.0 (http://creativecommons.org/licenses/by/2.0)], via Wikimedia Commons

Bio: Jason Rosette

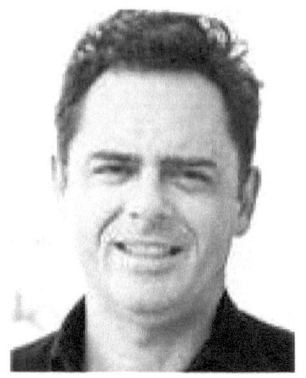

Writer/Director, Producer, Filmmaker, and Educator Jason Rosette works in a wide range of genres and media, alternating between features, documentaries, and commissioned entertainment and edutainment. His first feature, BookWars ("Terrific"-LA Times), was released in the year 2000 to wide critical acclaim, despite its guerilla-filmmaking origins. His debut dramatic feature as writer/director, the road movie Lost in New Mexico, was heralded by the Moving Arts Journal as "a unique and interesting take on the fluidity of technology versus the recurring commonality of the human condition".

Mr. Rosette has worked in Asia since 2004, and has produced numerous original and commissioned films and media in the region. There, Mr. Rosette-known also by his Asian aka 'Jack Ro'–wrote and directed the supernatural Vietnam War themed drama, Freedom Deal: Story of Lucky, while developing several future long form projects. Recently, he was working at the US Embassy in Rangoon (Yangon), Burma, American Center, while continuing to undertake a range of video and photography projects in the region.

Mr. Rosette is also a photographer, musician, and voiceover talent; he has acted in off-off Broadway in New York City and on numerous independent films, where he is often cast as an ambivalent 'seeker' character or as an agent or underworld figure.

BIO: WILLIAM GRABOWSKI

William Grabowski is the author of 8 books, most recently the techno-thriller Infinity Point, media tie-in Castro's Cadillac (from the screenplay by Michael Sayles), Amazon bestseller Black Light: Perspectives on Mysterious Phenomena, and Traces of Oblivion, a collection of best short stories including his 2004 novel The Untold, a horror/conspiracy thriller. Black Light was lauded by Emmy Award-winning investigative journalist George Knapp (KLAS/CBS-TV) as "A heck of a piece of work!" Grabowski's hundreds of articles, interviews and book reviews have been published on Forbes.com, Philadelphia Business Review, Hellnotes and elsewhere; and in magazines Beware the Dark, Cemetery Dance, National Public Radio-associated Wireless and many others.

Are you a Bootstrapper?

Contact Camerado Media to be a part of a future edition of The Bootstrapping Book Series at:

camerado@camerado.com

(c) Copyright 2016 - 2018 and beyond by Camerado and Jason Rosette

www.ingramcontent.com/pod-product-compliance
Lightning Source LLC
Chambersburg PA
CBHW031616210526
45464CB00004B/1597